Fault Lines

The New
UPDATED EDITION

Donald Liebich

Fault Lines

The New
UPDATED EDITION

*Understanding America's Role in the
Middle East and the Circumstances
Leading to the Rise of ISIS*

Donald Liebich

elevate

© 2016 by Don Liebich

Editorial Work by AnnaMarie McHargue
Cover Design by Arthur Cherry

Printed in the United States of America. All rights reserved under
International Copyright Law. Contents and/or cover may not be
reproduced in whole or in part in any form without the express
written consent of the publisher.

Published in Boise, Idaho by Elevate
www.elevatepub.com
info@elevatepub.com

ISBN 9781943425266
ISBN 9781943425600

NO TREES WERE HARMED IN THE MAKING OF THIS BOOK.
OK, so a few did need to make the ultimate sacrifice.
In order to steward our environment, we are partnered
with *Plant With Purpose*, to plant a tree for every tree
that paid the price for the printing of this book.

PLANT WITH PURPOSE I WWW.PLANTWITHPURPOSE.ORG

To learn more, visit wwwelevatepub.com/about

Every book is a collaboration of many sources. This is particularly true of Fault Lines, which, at its core, is the story of my personal journey. I, therefore, dedicate this work to my many friends and acquaintances in the Middle East who have inspired me with their hopes and dreams for a better and more peaceful life for their children.

Contents

Author's Note

In 2003, as I began the first of a series of trips to the Middle East, I discovered something curious: what I was seeing and learning in my travels generally did not correspond with what was being fed to me by U.S. media sources. As the discrepancies between what I observed and what I "knew" from home became more obvious, I began, in 2006, recording my thoughts and experiences as they related to the dynamics of the Middle East region. By writing and posting a regular blog on my site, *Memos from the Mountains*, I gave myself the opportunity to discern truth from fiction and to determine for myself what I actually believed was happening in Middle Eastern affairs. The blogs, along with comments offered by my readers, have proved to be a useful device as I work to understand all sides of what, at times, can be complex issues.

Many times during my trips through the region, I would hear comments such as, "We love Americans, but we hate your government and its policies," or, "We can forgive you for electing George Bush the first time. Everybody makes mistakes. But the second time, what were you thinking?" or "You are a democracy and you are responsible for your government." or "Why don't you rise up and overthrow your government?" I began to ask myself: How did the United States, a country that sees itself as "the shining city on the hill," or as "a beacon of freedom in the world," fall so far in the estimation of the people of this important region? In pursuit of answers to this question (and there is more than one), I began to study the history of American involvement in the Middle East and to reconcile that history with my own observations.

This book, therefore, is the story of a journey as reflected in my writings over the past seven years. In each chapter, as I examine the consequences of the fault lines that have run through United States-Middle East policy over the years, I will explain what I have concluded and how I reached that conclusion. I use the vehicle of the blogs as a commentary on events. In order to allow the reader to put my comments and thoughts in context, I have included the date of each posting. Although I have used the present tense to describe events, these are events that are now, in Middle Eastern terms, ancient history. I hope this vehicle allows the reader not only to see what I saw, but also to understand the journey that I have taken to reach my conclusions.

I also think it important to note that Arabic is a difficult language to transliterate into English. The Arabic language has a number of sounds that do not occur in English and, therefore, English language writers transcribe these sounds in a number of different ways. An example is the last name of the late, unlamented leader of Libya, *Muammar Qaddafi*. His name is variously translated as *Qaddafi, Gaddafi* or *al-Qaddafi*.

To deal with this issue, I have used the spelling that appears most often in news media and other sources. Where there is disagreement, I have used Wikipedia: Manual of Style/Arabic for guidance. In cases where Arabic names appear with different spelling in quotations, I have changed the spelling for purposes of consistency.

The reflections incorporated into this book are the result of ten trips to the Middle East over the last ten years. The trips, including economic and humanitarian projects, political trips, meetings with U.S. diplomats, government officials, nongovernmental organizations and non-state actors such as Hamas and Hezbollah, as well as religious pilgrimages, have framed my view of this part of the world. The friends that I have made in the region have kept me informed, providing their perspectives on current events. If you are interested in following my ongoing journey, it is available on www.donliebich.com.

Introduction

Looking back on the start of my career as a 23-year-old graduate in Chemical Engineering with a commission as an Ensign in the U.S. Navy, it is hard to imagine the journey that would unfold. Who knew that my path would include numerous trips to almost all of the countries in the Middle East and a fourth career spent trying to understand and explain the everchanging dynamics of this important region that, for decades, has vexed U.S. policymakers. During most of my Navy and business career, I had little interaction with people and countries outside of the United States. Having survived a brief interview with legendary Vice Admiral Hyman Rickover and trained in the Naval Nuclear Power program and Submarine Service, during my naval career, I served on attack submarines. The majority of our missions involved monitoring the activities of Soviet warships, including submarines, from the frigid waters off the coast of Russia. Except for a few R&R stops in Scotland and the Caribbean, the closest I got to a foreign country was viewing the coastline of Russia through a periscope from 12 miles away.

During those Cold War years, I never saw our adversaries in the Soviet Navy as hated enemies to be destroyed. For me, they were not part of the "Evil Empire" or an "Axis of Evil." Rather, they were competent professionals who, with inferior equipment, were trying to do the best job they could to serve their country. This view was reinforced many years later, when, while consulting in St. Petersburg, Russia, I had the opportunity to meet with an acquaintance and his wife over vodka and chocolate. In the course of the conversation, we discovered that we had both served in the nuclear submarine service and had patrolled in the same waters. It was entirely possible that some of our near collisions during the "cat and mouse" games of that time were with each other. Now we were really comrades, discussing our mutual hopes for ourselves and our children. This encounter has always been a reminder to me, when meeting with some of our adversaries in the Middle East, to try to see them as fathers and mothers, with the same hopes for a better life for their children that I have.

During my 25-year business career, I served as president of a distribution company that was one of the founding companies of Sysco Corporation. Again, in this capacity, I rarely looked beyond the borders of America. The global market was just emerging when I took early retirement. This insular outlook changed dramatically when I began a third career in international consulting for emerging economies. With this career I lived and worked in Russia, Eastern Europe, Indonesia and Venezuela. It was during this time that I had an experience that changed the way that I looked at our adversaries and the misleading way the U.S. government portrayed them.

My epiphany occurred in 1994 in St. Petersburg while I consulted with a Russian grocery store chain. During a meeting with the Vice President of Distribution about his vehicle acquisition practices, he told me that he could buy a Russianmade truck for 15,000 USD or a Volvo or Mercedes-Benz (MB) for 45,000 USD. He bought the Volvo or MB every time because it "would actually run and not break down every week."

Andrew Bacevich, author of *Washington Rules—America's Path to Permanent War*, retired U.S. Army Colonel, and Professor of International Relations and History at Boston University, took the same journey of discovery that I had taken. Although his journey started in a different place and at a different time, we ended up at the same destination. Professor Bacevich began his journey in 1990 when, as an active duty Army officer, he visited the German Democratic Republic and observed a Soviet military exercise. He not only noted that the trucks were 1950s vintage, but also saw with his own eyes one of their battle tanks suddenly belch smoke and burst into flames.

Like Professor Bacevich, I had been indoctrinated during my military career that we were faced off against the vaunted Soviet military machine that posed an existential threat to the U.S. and its allies and required enormous expenditures for personnel, armaments and foreign bases. I asked myself, *How had I not realized the fact that the Soviet Union was nothing more than a "paper tiger"?* In reality, it was an adversary that, at first glance, appeared to be strong, but underneath was weak and unable to exert influence or defend its interests.

My introduction to the Middle East began when friends with a small U.S. NGO working in Jordan invited me to visit Jordan, in order to see the results of their efforts in small rural villages there. I became interested in what they had accomplished and returned twice more to help build Habitat for Humanity houses in these villages. Approximately one half of the population of Jordan is made up of Palestinians, most of whom are refugees from the 1948 and 1967 Arab-Israeli wars. While in Jordan, I visited refugee camps and learned all that I could about their lives and histories. I was surprised to find that these stories did not match the information fed to me by American media sources. In fact, as I went deeper, I realized that I, as an average American, really had little idea as to what was taking place in the Middle East.

As I began to review the history of American involvement in the Middle East, I saw several themes emerge. One is that U.S. efforts to project power in the region have clashed with the desire of Middle Easterners for political independence. The United States also has had difficulty in dealing with conflicting interests and objectives that, many times, are mutually exclusive. In addition, the U.S. has failed to recognize or deal with the long-term, unintended consequences of its policies and actions. In many cases, the U.S. simply has failed to achieve its foreign policy objectives. In other cases, the U.S. may have accomplished its goals but only *in spite of* its policies rather than *because of* its policies—and these rare successes have tended to cause problems down the road. As we examine events in the first decades of the 21st century, we will find a waning of U.S. ability to influence events and a growing view in the region that the world's hegemon is, itself, no more than a "paper tiger." This book will explain the fault lines that have run through American Middle East policies over the years and demonstrate how those policies have led to the United States' declining influence in the region. I also propose steps that might be taken to reverse the trend.

Fault Lines begins with a brief history of American involvement in the Middle East and American policies in the region and is intended to give the reader an historical framework for understanding contemporary issues. When Americans use the phrase "that's history," the implication is that it is irrelevant. Throughout many regions of the world, and especially the Middle East, history is everything. Middle Easterners can remember exactly why they are mad at the United States, while Americans, on the other hand, are serial amnesiacs. We know that we are supposed to be mad at a country; we just can't remember why.

Chapter 3 looks at how America's effort to project power has clashed with the Middle Eastern desire for political independence. Chapter 4 examines the unintended consequences of American involvement and policies and how these consequences, in many cases, only have made the situation worse. Chapter 5 addresses how the U.S. desire for stability has clashed with its goal of promoting democracy. In Chapter 6 we look at the decline of American influence as a result of domestic, global and regional factors. Chapter 7 examines the other regional state and non-state actors, including Israel, Iran and other competing influences, that have arisen to challenge American dominance on the Middle Eastern stage. In Chapter 8 we review the global resurgence and rising power of new players, such as Russia, Turkey, China and others. And finally, in Chapter 9, I propose some suggestions as to how the United States can restore its credibility and influence in the Middle East.

Throughout this work, I make no claim to academic training on Middle Eastern history or politics. What I have learned, I have learned from interacting with people in all walks of life during my many trips and by reading many publications and articles by correspondents and experts in the United States, Europe and the Middle East. I am extremely grateful to Dr. Salim Yaqub, Professor of History (with a focus on the Middle East) at the University of California, Santa Barbara, for his insights. Dr. Yaqub's Teaching Company course, *The United States and the Middle East: 1914 to 9/11*, has been invaluable to me, both in understanding the historical role of the United States in the Middle East and in framing the issues that have plagued U.S. policymakers in the past and, in many cases, still today.

These issues can be complex, confusing and rapidly changing. My goal in writing was and is not to break new scholarly ground or create a comprehensive treatise on any of the issues. Instead, my goal is to provide a resource for thoughtful Americans who are interested in a better understanding of the stories behind the headlines. I leave it to the reader whose interest is sufficiently piqued to dig deeper into the complexity of the issues.

Timeline of United States–Middle East Involvement

1914   World War I begins; Turkey joins the war on the side of Germany and Austria.

1915   Turkey crushes an Armenian revolt.

1917   Great Britain issues the Balfour Declaration; U.S. enters WWI.

1918   World War I ends; Britain and France divide up the Ottoman Empire into spheres of influence; U.S. rejects a mandate over Armenia.

1933   Adolf Hitler comes to power in Germany.

1939   World War II begins.

1941   United States enters WWII and joins Britain and France in occupying Iran.

1945   WWII ends.

1947   President Harry Truman issues the Truman Doctrine; UN General Assembly passes Resolution 181, the Palestine Partition Plan.

1948   Israel declares independence; first Arab-Israeli War begins.

1949   Armistice ends the Arab-Israeli War.

1951   Iran begins the nationalization of its oil industry.

1953   CIA overthrows the Iranian Prime Minister, Mohammad Mosaddegh.

1956   Egyptian President Gamal Nasser nationalizes the Suez Canal Company; Suez War occurs.

1957   President Eisenhower issues the Eisenhower Doctrine.

1958   Political unrest begins in Lebanon; U.S. Marines intervene in Lebanon.

1962   Yemen civil war begins.

1963   President Kennedy is assassinated.

1964   Palestine Liberation Organization (PLO) is established.

1965   Ayatollah Ruhollah Khomeini is expelled from Iran.

1967   Arab-Israeli Six-Day War occurs.

1969   President Nixon issues the Nixon Doctrine.

1969-70   Egypt-Israel War of Attrition occurs.

1970   Black September Crisis occurs; Anwar Sadat becomes President of Egypt.

1973   Yom Kippur War occurs.

1978   Egypt and Israel conclude the Camp David Agreement; Iranian Revolution begins.

1979   Mohammad Reza Shah Pahlavi leaves Iran; Ayatollah Khomeini returns to Iran; Egypt and Israel sign peace treaty; Iran hostage crisis begins; Soviet Union invades Afghanistan.

1980   President Carter issues the Carter Doctrine; Iran-Iraq War begins; Operation Cyclone (Charlie Wilson's War) begins in Afghanistan.

1981   Iran frees the U.S. hostages; Egypt President Anwar Sadat is assassinated.

1982   Israel invades Lebanon; Sabra-Shatila massacres occur: U.S. Marines land in Lebanon.

1983   Truck bomb kills 241 U.S. Marines in Lebanon.

1984   President Reagan withdraws the Marines from Lebanon.

1984-85 U.S. sells arms to Iran in exchange for the release of hostages.

1987   First Palestinian *Intifada* breaks out in the West Bank and Gaza.

1988   Iran-Iraq War ends; U.S. begins dialogue with the PLO.

1989   Soviet Union withdraws from Afghanistan; Osama bin-Laden forms al-Qaeda.

1990   Iraq invades Kuwait.

1991   First Gulf War occurs.

1992   Pro-Soviet government in Afghanistan falls; Afghan factions begin to fight among themselves.

1993   First World Trade Center bombing occurs; Israel and PLO sign the Oslo Accords.

1996   Taliban take power in Afghanistan; Osama bin Laden returns to Afghanistan and calls for *jihad* against the United States.

1998   Al-Qaeda operatives bomb U.S. embassies in Kenya and Tanzania.

2000   Israel-Palestine summit at Camp David fails; Second Palestinian *Intifada* begins.

2001   Al-Qaeda terrorists attack the World Trade Center and the Pentagon; President Bush issues the Bush Doctrine; U.S. invades Afghanistan.

2002   President Bush identifies Iraq, Iran and North Korea as "Axis of Evil" in his State of the Union Address.

2003   U.S. invades Iraq, topples the Saddam Hussein-led government and bans all members of the Ba'ath Party from any public sector jobs.

2005   Iraq holds its first election and President Bush promises to "foster democracy in every nation and culture."

2006   Hamas wins the Palestinian Authority (PA) election. The U.S. refuses to recognize it and cuts off aid to the PA. Israel attacks and invades Gaza and Lebanon.

2007   U.S. deploys 20,000 more troops in Iraq.

2008   Israel attacks and invades Gaza.

2009   U.S. and coalition forces begin to withdraw from Iraq.

2010   A series of popular uprisings begin in the Middle East and North Africa, which topple governments in Tunisia, Egypt, Libya and Yemen. U.S. combat troops complete withdrawal from Iraq.

2011   France, the U.S. and the United Kingdom intervene in Libya and force President Muammar Gaddafi from power. Uprisings in Syria turn violent and the Syrian Civil War begins. U.S. begins aid to the Free Syrian Army rebel group. Saudi Arabia and UAE intervene in Bahrain to assist in a crackdown on Shia protesters.

2013   NATO begins withdrawal of troops from Afghanistan. A military coup in Egypt deposes elected President Mohamed Morsi. The EU3+3 begin negotiations with Iran about its nuclear program.

2014   NATO officially ends its combat role in Afghanistan. The Islamic State in Iraq and al-Shams (ISIS) conquers large swaths of territory in Iraq and Syria and declares an Islamic caliphate. Israel attacks and invades Gaza.

2015   Saudi Arabia and UAE intervene in Yemen Civil War on behalf of the internationally recognized government. EU3+3 and Iran reach an agreement on a Joint Comprehensive Plan of Action (JCPOA) on Iran's nuclear program.

CHAPTER I

America's Increasing Engagement

From Harry Truman to Richard Nixon

The Middle East/North Africa is one area of the world in which a brief history of American involvement is possible. Except for interventions brought about by the First and Second Barbary Wars in the late 1700s and early 1800s and the Moroccan Crisis of 1905-1906, the U.S. through its early history had little interest in the politics of the Middle East. For centuries, prior to the end of World War I, the Middle East and parts of North Africa and Europe were under the control of the Ottoman Empire. But, by the early 20th century the Ottoman Empire was an empire more in name than in substance. Direct central control rarely extended very far from the Sublime Porte, the seat of government in Constantinople, now Istanbul. Most of the modern day Middle East, from the Arabian Desert to the Taurus Mountains in Turkey, was ruled as the Province of Syria with its seat of government in Damascus. These quasi-independent rulers held sway in most of the outlying provinces. As long as they didn't skim too much off of their remittances to Constantinople, the Sublime Porte largely left them alone. American undertakings were mostly aimed at protecting the lives and property of American citizens. Compared to Britain and France, who either annexed or occupied a number of Ottoman provinces, for most Middle Easterners, the Americans seemed like the good guys.

Benign Neglect Diminishes

This period of benign neglect began to wane with the advent of World War I and the political disruptions that ensued. During and immediately after World War I, three issues drew the U.S. more deeply into Middle Eastern politics. The first issue involved the Turkish government's brutal crushing of the 1915 Armenian revolt in what is now called the Armenian Genocide. The Armenians are Christian and American missionaries in the U.S. conducted a massive campaign to call attention to the plight of the Armenians and to turn the U.S. government against the Muslim Ottomans. This anti-Muslim sentiment played a role in the U.S. acquiescence to British and French efforts to break up the Ottoman Empire.

The second issue involving the U.S. in Middle Eastern politics was Zionism. In 1917 the British government was persuaded to issue The Balfour Declaration which called for "the establishment in Palestine of a national home for the Jewish people." Supreme Court Justice Louis Brandeis, a Zionist Jew, urged President Woodrow Wilson to support the declaration. His support helped to encourage the British government to issue the declaration.

The third issue was European Imperialism. President Wilson was eager that the war, and the American involvement in it, not be seen through the lens of imperialist ambitions. This hope was destroyed when the Bolshevik government in Russia, which had withdrawn from the war and portrayed it as an imperialist conflict, discovered the secret **Sykes-Picot** agreement in Czech archives and publicized it. The agreement outlined a British/French plan to divide up the Ottoman Empire after the war. The mandates set up by the agreement were eventually approved by the League of Nations and subsequently divided Middle Eastern territories into British and French spheres of influence. The Ottoman Province of Syria was divided by the French into Lebanon and Syria and by the British into Iraq, Transjordan and Palestine. The borders were designed to keep the indigenous populations divided in order to facilitate the colonial governance of the territories. These

Sykes-Picot, officially known as the **Asia Minor Agreement**, was a secret 1916 agreement between the governments of the United Kingdom and France defining their proposed spheres of influence and control in the Middle East following World War I.

artificial borders have been largely maintained for the modern states of the region.

President Wilson initially pushed back against this imperial agenda, articulating a policy of self-determination. But the combination of Wilson's poor health and the reemergence of isolationism in the United States following the bloody war ensured the failure of his policy. The resulting treaties and agreements, for the most part, played out the way Britain and France had planned. By 1922, the U.S. had reverted to a hands-off policy and maintained this stance for the next decade. During the 1930s the growth of Zionism in the U.S. and an increasing demand for oil began to change perceptions of the importance of the Middle East.

Middle East Becomes Vital U.S. Interest

During the period of World War II, the U.S., for the first time, saw the geopolitical orientation of Middle East countries as a vital national interest. We also see the beginnings of the kind of dilemmas created by objectives that are conflicting and at times mutually exclusive. Wartime concerns made it imperative to deny control of the region to the Axis powers, thereby maintaining open supply lines to the Soviet Union, and ensuring Allied access to the region's oil reserves. These objectives conflicted with the default U.S. policy of supporting the national ambitions of countries struggling to free themselves from European colonial domination. In a time of war, the imperative of defeating the Axis powers took precedence.

The Allies were concerned about Iranian leader Reza Shah Pahlavi's neutrality and alleged pro-German leanings. In order to accomplish their wartime objectives, Britain and the Soviet Union, supported by the U.S., invaded and occupied Iran. They forced Reza Shah to abdicate in favor of his more compliant son, Mohammad Reza Shah Pahlavi. The Allies then established Iran as a supply corridor to the Soviet Union. The U.S. extended diplomatic recognition and aid to Saudi Arabia in order to secure oil supplies and bribed and pressured Turkey to remain neutral. The Allies did not want Turkey to join the war on the Allied side, as they would then have to defend Turkey if it were attacked by Germany. On the other hand if Turkey sided with Germany and closed the Turkish Straits, the Soviet Union would be cut off from the Mediterranean Sea. When Egypt seemed on the verge of installing a pro-German government, the U.S. supported British military action in order to ensure that a pro-British government was installed.

Following the defeat of the Axis powers in 1945, the Soviet Union quickly emerged as the new adversary for the U.S. and its western allies. While, at that time, the U.S. did not require Middle Eastern oil, its European allies did. The U.S., therefore, began to see stability that would ensure unfettered access to the region's oil supplies as a vital national interest. Despite the growing U.S. interest, Britain, with its long history in the region, remained the dominant power. The U.S. was content to allow Britain to take the lead in dealing with Middle East issues.

World War II, however, militarily and financially weakened Britain, and it soon became apparent that the nation was no longer capable of being the guarantor of Middle East stability. This realization, combined with confrontations with the Soviet Union in Turkey and Iran, led to the promulgation of the so-called Truman Doctrine. The doctrine stated, "It must be the policy of the United States to support free peoples who are resisting attempted subjugation by armed minorities or by outside pressure." For better or for worse, this statement guided U.S. Cold War policies for over a generation.

In order to help ensure oil availability, the Truman administration made a formal pledge to defend the Kingdom of Saudi Arabia should it be attacked by the Soviet Union. The Treasury Department also issued a tax credit regulation, referred to as the "Golden Gimmick," which made it easier for Aramco, the American oil company consortium, to do business in Saudi Arabia by sharing profits 50/50. As we shall see, this arrangement would soon come back to haunt the U.S. and Britain in Iran. In addition to oil, the Truman administration grew concerned about Syria's anti-Israel stance, its border disputes with Turkey and the increasing leftist, pro-Soviet policies of Syrian President Shukri al-Quwatli. In order to deal with these concerns, the CIA helped orchestrate the overthrow of the Quwatli government by the Syrian military. The overthrow led to a series of military coups and years of unstable governments in Syria. Thus the U.S. began a policy of intervening directly in the Middle East as a means of shaping the geopolitical landscape to its liking.

Creation of the State of Israel

No event has been more surrounded in myth or has had more influence on U.S. policy and involvement in the Middle East from 1948 until the present or has done more to embitter the Arab world against the United States than the creation of the state of Israel. This event is known to Arab Palestinians as the **"Nakba,"** or catastrophe. Napoleon Bonaparte's comment that "history is myth agreed upon" certainly applies in this case with historians publishing at least two versions of the story.

Nakba (literally "catastrophe" in Arabic) refers to the destruction of Palestinian society with the founding of the State of Israel in 1948 when approximately 750,000 Palestinians fled or were forced into exile by Israeli troops.

The Nazi Holocaust during World War II increased Zionist pressure on Britain for a Jewish homeland in Palestine. Britain resisted this pressure, fearing an Arab backlash that would jeopardize the flow of oil to their struggling post-war economy. This resistance prompted Jewish militias in Palestine, such as the Haganah and the Irgun, to step up their military and terrorist campaign against British forces. In 1946 the Irgun bombed the British military and diplomatic headquarters in the King David Hotel resulting in the deaths of 90 people, many of them civilians. By early 1947, Britain had had enough and turned the problem over to the United Nations.

The Passage of Resolution 181

The UN formed a special Palestine Commission that recommended partition of Palestine into Jewish and Arab states. On November 29, 1947, the UN General Assembly adopted this plan in the form of **Resolution 181**. Interestingly, the Resolution was supported by the United States (despite State Department opposition), Britain and their allies as well as the Soviet Union and its allies. The Soviets felt that

Resolution 181 was passed by the United Nations in 1947 and called for the partition of Palestine into Arab and Jewish states, with the city of Jerusalem as a separate entity to be governed by a special international regime. The resolution—which was considered by the Jewish community in Palestine to be a legal basis for the establishment of Israel, and which was rejected by the Arab community—was succeeded almost immediately by violence.

a Jewish state, largely populated by European Jews, many of whom were Socialists, if not outright Communists, would act as a buffer state against British imperialism in the region. President Truman's Zionist advisers, Clark Clifford and David Niles, coerced many unaligned states into voting for the Resolution. The Arab states all opposed the Resolution feeling that the plan punished Arabs and Muslims by forcing them to give up their land in atonement for the sins of European Christians during the Nazi Holocaust. The Resolution contained many provisions designed to protect the rights of the indigenous Arabs, both Muslim and Christian, and these provisions were to be implemented by October 1, 1948.

Following the passage of Resolution 181, unrest and violence increased dramatically in Palestine. Irregular Arab militias clashed with Jewish militias and both sides conducted terrorist attacks resulting in many casualties, both civilian and military. The most notorious event occurred in the Arab village of Deir Yassin, outside of Jerusalem, when the Irgun invaded the village and massacred over 100 Arabs including many women and children. The process of implementing Resolution 181 was preempted on May 14, 1948 when Jewish leaders unilaterally declared the independent state of Israel. Within a few hours, President Truman, for both humanitarian and domestic political considerations, accorded diplomatic recognition to the Jewish state.

Initially, the Arab states were reluctant to get involved in the conflict militarily. However, faced with popular pressure from their own citizens following reports of massacres such as that at Deir Yassin, a flood of refugees evicted by the Jewish militias and incensed by the Jewish declaration of an independent state, on May 15[th,] the Arab states attacked the new state. The conflict lasted until early 1949 when an armistice agreement ended the fighting and established new borders that are now referred to as the 1967 borders or the Green Line.

U.S. Influence Declines

The armistice largely held, but the Arab states refused to recognize the new state of Israel. President Truman was unhappy with the behavior of Israel after the war and tried to persuade Israel to repatriate the refugees. Israel refused and eventually Truman gave up. Clearly the Truman administration played an important role in bringing the Jewish state into existence and displacing the existing Arab population. Following these events U.S. influence and image in the Middle East declined drastically.

With the arrival of the Eisenhower administration in 1953, the **Cold War** with the Soviet Union continued to be the primary lens through which the U.S. saw foreign policy issues. The need to contain the Soviet Union became the focus of most foreign policy decisions. However, the lingering vestiges of European imperialism remained as an impediment to efforts to enlist Middle Eastern countries into the western camp of the Cold War. The CIA-orchestrated coup that overthrew democratically elected Iranian Prime Minister Mohammad Mosaddegh in 1953 helped to persuade

The *Cold War* was a sustained state of political and military tension between powers in the Western Bloc (the United States with NATO and others) and powers in the Eastern Bloc (the Soviet Union and its allies in the Warsaw Pact). Historians have not fully agreed on the dates, but 1947–1991 is common.

middle easterners that the U.S. belonged firmly in the western imperialist group. As Iranian nationalism grew, the Iranian government was pushing the Anglo-Iranian Oil Company. (AIOC) for the same 50/50 profit split that was in place in Saudi Arabia and Venezuela, among others. Unable to reach an agreement, the Iranian parliament, led by Mosaddegh, nationalized the AIOC. The British responded by imposing an embargo on Iranian oil and advocating for military intervention. The Truman administration had opposed military action.

The Eisenhower administration, however, saw Mosaddegh's radical policies, which included opposition to the western backed shah, as threatening to regional stability by opening the way for Soviet intervention. Eisenhower was, therefore, more favorable toward American intervention.

The CIA dispatched Kermit Roosevelt to Iran. Roosevelt colluded with local opposition and the Iranian military to stage a military coup to replace Mosaddegh with a pro-shah prime minister. U.S. officials, who saw this overthrow as a great victory, did not take into account the unintended consequences. Ordinary Iranians came to see the shah as a despotic American puppet. These perceptions were manifested in the Iranian revolution of 1979.

U.S. Imperialism Fuels Arab Nationalism

Perceptions of the U.S. as an imperial power were also a major cause of the rise of Arab nationalism, led by Egyptian President **Gamal Abdel Nasser**. Nasser was a charismatic and forceful advocate for Arab nationalism and resistance to western domination. In an effort to stem Nasser's drift toward the Soviet Bloc, the U.S. advocated a more evenhanded position with respect to the Arab-Israeli conflict. In practice, however, this only meant pushing for an Egyptian/Israeli peace agreement and an agreement on the post-1949 borders rather than a return to the UN partition borders. Balancing efforts to retain the oil-rich Arab countries in the western camp with staunch U.S. support for Israel soon became an almost impossible task and the U.S. reverted to a more hardline approach to dealing with Egypt. Specifically, the U.S. curtailed its aid to Egypt, reneged on its agreement to fund the Aswan Dam and encouraged other western countries to provide military equipment to Israel.

The 1956 Suez Crisis brought about a sea-change in the Middle East balance of power. After the U.S. withdrew its offer to finance the Aswan Dam, Nasser nationalized the Suez Canal saying that he would use the

President **Gamal Abdel Nasser** was the second President of the Republic of Egypt following the overthrow of the monarchy in 1952, serving from 1956 until his death in 1970.

toll revenues from the canal to finance the dam. In response, Britain began to mobilize a military effort to reclaim the canal and overthrow Nasser. In October 1956, Israel, Britain and France attacked Egypt after concocting a subterfuge under which Israel would attack Egypt. Once Israel had seized the Sinai Peninsula, Britain and France would then demand that Israel and Egypt withdraw from the canal area, a demand that Egypt was sure to refuse. Britain and France would then seize the canal ostensibly to protect it from war damage.[1] This subterfuge was so blatantly absurd that it fooled no one. Eisenhower, who had opposed military action, quickly threatened to cut off western oil supplies to Europe, to refuse to guarantee British debt and to impose sanctions on Israel. The threats worked and the three invading countries withdrew. (Israel remained in the Sinai until March 1957 and destroyed much of the infrastructure before withdrawing.)

The Eisenhower Doctrine

This episode made it clear that Britain could no longer function as the primary western power in the Middle East and assume the task of standing up for western interests against Soviet influence. In response to this changed reality, President Eisenhower did what any American president would do. He promulgated the "Eisenhower Doctrine." The resolution, among other things, declared the intention of the U.S. to provide aid to Middle Eastern countries and to intervene militarily to protect any Middle Eastern country that was a victim of "overt armed aggression from any country controlled by International Communism." While it was never clear exactly what this meant in practice, the Eisenhower administration hoped that it would encourage countries of the region to ally with the west against the Soviet Union and its Middle Eastern allies, Syria and Egypt.

This "take it or leave it" approach put Arab regimes in a difficult position. Popular opinion strongly supported Nasser and his Syria/Egypt Pan-Arab movement. Their governments, however, were anxious to receive the promised U.S. aid. The pro-western regimes in Jordan and Saudi Arabia, bowing to domestic pressure, declined to endorse the doctrine publically, but they managed to persuade the U.S. to provide the aid anyway. Only two Arab governments, Lebanon and Iraq, publically aligned themselves with the U.S. In Lebanon this decision helped ignite a civil war between pro-western Maronite Christians and pro-Nasser Muslims. The civil war was quelled when the U.S. intervened by dispatching 1,400 Marines to Lebanon. The U.S. then orchestrated the selection of a consensus presidential candidate Fuad Chehab. Chehab followed a path of moderation and promptly backed away from endorsing the Eisenhower doctrine.

Iraq's endorsement of the doctrine triggered a military coup by the so-called Free Officers who tended to favor Nasser's Pan-Arab agenda. The bloody coup overthrew the pro-western monarchy of Hashemite King Faisal II and resulted in the gruesome deaths of Faisal and many members of his family.

Salim Yaqub, of the University of California, Santa Barbara, points out, "The objective (of the Eisenhower Doctrine) was to prevent a Soviet takeover of the Middle East and given that such a takeover never occurred, it has to be said that the objective was achieved. The strategy to achieve the objective, discrediting Arab figures deemed to be 'soft on communism' by promoting other Arab figures, who were conspicuously anticommunist, failed miserably."[2]

Egyptian President Gamal Nasser, bemused by the whole affair, famously commented to an American CIA friend, "The genius of you Americans is that you never make clear-cut stupid moves, only complicated stupid moves which make the rest of us wonder at the possibility that we might be missing something."

Kennedy Attempts Balance

When John F. Kennedy came to power in 1961, he abandoned the Eisenhower Doctrine and moved away from a Cold War view of Middle East issues. He attempted to improve relations with Arab nationalists and respect their foreign policy choices. This position, however, had its own internal contradictions as Kennedy had to balance support for Arab nationalists while maintaining relations with conservative Arab monarchies. These contradictions came to a head in 1962 when a civil war broke out in Yemen. Egypt supported the republican government while Saudi Arabia supported the monarchists. The civil war evolved into a proxy war between Egypt and Saudi Arabia that eventually would have a strong impact on Egypt's 1967 war with Israel. Kennedy's attempt at balance made neither side happy and both accused the U.S. of supporting the other side.

Kennedy also tried to improve relations with Israel, which had been somewhat testy during the Eisenhower administration. Kennedy took this position, not only for domestic political reasons, but also from a belief that, if Israel felt secure, it would be more likely to compromise on issues that would contribute to overall Middle East stability. To that end, Kennedy sold Israel advanced weaponry and wanted Israel to allow the return of refugees from the 1948 war and to refrain from developing a nuclear weapon. Kennedy, however, never made a formal linkage and, therefore, Israel took the weaponry and continued to develop a nuclear weapon and deny any return of refugees.

In Iran, Kennedy pushed the shah to moderate his repressive policies and to institute reforms, which would placate the growing opposition movement. The shah responded by instituting some electoral and land reforms. These reforms alienated almost everybody; the leftist students because they didn't go far enough and the conservative clerics because they controlled much of the land. By the time of his assassination in 1963, most of Kennedy's initiatives had been thwarted and when Lyndon Johnson assumed the presidency, the initiatives were abandoned.

Johnson Allies U.S. with Iran

The Johnson administration returned to the policy of uncritical support for the Shah of Iran that had characterized U.S./Iranian relations under the Eisenhower administration. Pressure on the shah to implement internal reforms essentially ceased and the U.S. sold massive amounts of modern weapons to the shah's military. As a result of the U.S. support for the shah and his repressive policies, the Iranian public opposed the U.S./Iran relationship. The shah's security services arrested, jailed, tortured and, in some cases, deported opposition leaders. One such leader was a little known cleric, Ayatollah Ruhollah Khomeini. Khomeini would return in triumph following the revolution in 1979. Ironically, as Iranian oil revenues increased during the 1960s and 70s, U.S. influence on Iran actually declined.

Under Johnson, relations with Egypt grew even worse. With his frail ego, Johnson reacted with great affront to Nasser's bombastic diatribes; diatribes that Kennedy mostly ignored. The result was that Nasser and Johnson developed great personal enmity, which spilled over into U.S. policy, as the U.S. reduced aid and drew closer to the conservative monarchies of the region.

The Six-Day War

When it came to Israel, Johnson quickly abandoned any pretense of balance, saying to an Israeli diplomat shortly after Kennedy's death, "You have lost a very great friend, but you have found an even greater one."[3] The Johnson administration sold vast quantities of weapons to Israel, including, for the first time, weapons with offensive capabilities. As the 1960s neared the end, the Johnson administration was preoccupied with the domestic and global implications of the Vietnam War. As Johnson was trying to focus on Southeast Asia, the "Six-Day War" between Israel and its Arab neighbors broke out in 1967 and changed the strategic and political landscape in the Middle East forever.

1948 Arab–Israeli War, or the **First Arab–Israeli War**, was fought between the State of Israel and a military coalition of Arab states and Palestinian Arab forces. This war was the second stage of the 1948 Palestine war or the Nakba (the Catastrophe).

Like the **1948 Arab-Israeli War**, the 1967 Arab-Israeli War (Six-Day War) is surrounded in myths that do more to obfuscate the situation than to clarify it. In order to understand the context for these events, one must go back to 1956 and the end of the Suez Crisis. At the end of that war, Egypt made two concessions. It ended its blockade of Israeli shipping through the Straits of Tiran, a narrow strait between the Gulf of Aqaba and the Red Sea through which Israeli shipping from Eilat, Israel's only Red Sea port must pass. It also agreed to end cross border raids into Israeli territory. In order to guarantee the agreements, a UN Peacekeeping Force was stationed in the Sinai and in the Gaza Strip.

Arab World Divided

By 1967, the Arab world was divided into two mutually antagonistic camps. The conservative monarchies, such as Jordan and Saudi Arabia, were in one pro-American camp. The radical camp, consisting of Egypt, Syria and Iraq, tended to be more pro-Soviet. Each side accused the other of being soft on the Palestinian issue and conducted a venomous war of words. Egypt and Saudi Arabia were engaged in a proxy war in Yemen, which tied up as many as 70,000 Egyptian troops.

In May 1967 Egyptian President Gamal Nasser requested the removal of the UN peacekeepers from the Sinai. His motives appear to have been twofold. One, he wanted to be in a better position to defend Egypt in the event of an Israeli attack, which the Soviets had falsely told him was coming. Two, he wanted to placate critics who accused him of hiding behind the peacekeepers in order to avoid conflict with Israel. After the peacekeepers departed and Egypt reoccupied the Sinai, Nasser could no longer use the UN as an excuse for inaction. Nasser came under enormous pressure, both domestically and regionally to close the Straits of Tiran. While the Straits of Tiran were not a major commercial issue for Israel, Israel had drawn a red line requiring military action if Egypt closed the straits. While he realized that closure risked war with Israel, for which he was completely unprepared, his need to save face in the region compelled him to go forward with the closure.

Israel Strikes

The Johnson administration, fearing that the U.S. might be drawn into an Israeli-Arab war, asked Israel to refrain from firing the first shot in order to allow time to assemble an international flotilla to challenge the blockade. Israel agreed. On the Egyptian side, the Soviet Union told Nasser that they could not come to his aid and Nasser agreed not to fire the first shot. Although Nasser was now in a defensive posture, his rhetoric and that of other Arab leaders was extremely bellicose. This rhetoric terrified the Israeli public and the government was under strong public pressure to do something. The U.S. was having difficulty organizing the flotilla and in conversations with the Israelis left the impression that, while they hoped to avoid war, they no longer would object to Israel firing the first shot.

At the same time, the Israeli generals were pressing the cabinet to authorize a preemptive strike on Egypt. The generals felt that Egypt was not ready for war and would not be for over a year. If Israel struck first, they could destroy the Egyptian army. The fact that the army was in the Sinai only made it easier. The cabinet agreed and, on June 5, 1967, Israel launched a surprise air attack on Egypt and destroyed its air force on the ground. By evening, the Israelis had also destroyed the Jordanian and Syrian air forces.

Deprived of air cover and poorly led, the Egyptian army was quickly defeated and Israel occupied the Sinai Peninsula. When Jordan and Syria entered the war, Israel captured the West Bank including East Jerusalem and then took the Golan Plateau from Syria. By the time a ceasefire was declared on June 11, Israel had tripled the territory under its control. President Johnson's reaction to the Israeli attack on Egypt in 1967 was quite different from Eisenhower's in 1956. Eisenhower had insisted in the ceasefire agreement that Israel withdraw from the occupied territories. Johnson, however, called for "a cease fire in place" which allowed Israel to retain the occupied territories indefinitely.

The Six-Day War was a devastating defeat for Nasser's secular pan-Arab movement. The decline of secular nationalism left a political vacuum that began to be filled by Palestinian nationalism and political Islam. These two movements would create a whole new set of challenges for U.S. Middle East policy makers.

The Nixon Doctrine

As the Nixon administration arrived on the scene in 1969, policy makers not only had to deal with Middle East issues, but were also faced with a war in Vietnam that was rapidly becoming a quagmire. The American public had soured on military adventures around the globe making future foreign interventions difficult. In addition, America's economic supremacy was being challenged by Japan and Western Europe, which had recovered from the devastation of WWII. Faced with these realities, Nixon articulated, in an address in November, policies that came to be known as the Nixon Doctrine. It stated,

- First, the United States will keep all of its treaty commitments.

- Second, we shall provide a shield if a nuclear power threatens the freedom of a nation allied with us or of a nation whose survival we consider vital to our security.

- Third, in cases involving other types of aggression, we shall furnish military and economic assistance when requested in accordance with our treaty commitments. But we shall look to the nation directly threatened to assume the primary responsibility of providing the man-power for its defense.[4]

The practical effect of this strategy was that the U.S. needed to rely on strong regional allies who would protect American interests. In the Middle East, Iran and Saudi Arabia became the "twin pillars" of American policy. In order to support this policy the U.S. gave vast amounts of military aid to Iran and ignored the shah's human rights violations. This aid, both in the form of advanced equipment and financial resources, made Iran the strongest military power in the region; a situation that played right into the shah's ambitions of regional domination. Saudi Arabia, flush with petrodollars, was able to purchase billions of dollars of arms from American defense contractors.

The War of Attrition

Tensions between Israel and its Arab neighbors increased in early 1969 with both Israel and Egypt conducting cross border attacks in what came to be known as "The War of Attrition." In December 1969, Secretary of State William Rogers proposed a major Israeli-Arab peace initiative known as the "Roger's Plan." He proposed a land for peace arrangement in which Israel would withdraw from most of the territory occupied in 1967 in return for peace and recognition by the Arab states. Both sides rejected the proposal and the War of Attrition

The *Palestinian Liberation Organization* was founded in May 1964 by the Arab League in order to unite the groups opposed to the State of Israel. Its goal was to create an independent State of Palestine.

continued. Out of this maelstrom, a new player emerged, the **Palestinian Liberation Organization (PLO)**.

The Emergence of the PLO

Following the 1967 war, the PLO had essentially established a state within a state in Jordan. After numerous attempts to assassinate King Hussein of Jordan, in September 1970 the PLO hijacked five airliners from various European cities and Bahrain and landed them in Jordan and Egypt. In an event that came to be known by the PLO as "Black September." (A group named for this event would be heard from at the Munich Olympics in 1972.) King Hussein, seeing this as a threat to Jordanian sovereignty, attacked PLO headquarters in an effort to evict the Palestinians. When Syria tried to come to the aid of the Palestinians, Hussein asked the U.S. for assistance. The U.S., bogged down in Asia, and in no position to respond, asked Israel to come to Jordan's aid. Israel's show of force compelled Syria to withdraw and Hussein succeeded in evicting the PLO.

The Nixon administration was pleased with Israel's performance and made Israel the third pillar of U.S. policy (the two others still being Saudi Arabia and Iran) in the Middle East, lavishing millions of dollars of military and economic aid on Israel. These events further persuaded Nixon that the Middle East was politically a "no win" situation and he tried to maintain an arm's length policy. As with many foreign policy issues that American presidents would like to ignore, the issues have a way of finding them.

On October 6, 1973, Anwar Sadat, now President of Egypt, determined to recover the land lost in the 1967 war, launched a surprise attack on Israel. (Yom Kippur War) Sadat's territorial objectives were modest, but his larger diplomatic objective was to send a message to the Soviet Union and the U.S. that they could not ignore Egypt. Caught by surprise and attacked by both Egypt and Syria, Israel was in serious jeopardy and called on the U.S. for assistance.

With President Nixon paralyzed by the Watergate affair, **Henry Kissinger** managed the U.S. response. Kissinger saw the situation through a Cold War lens and was determined to keep the Soviet Union from increasing its influence in the Middle East. While orchestrating a massive arms airlift to shore up Israel, Kissinger wanted to prevent a complete humiliation of Egypt, which would drive it into the Soviet camp. By directly mediating the Israel-Egypt disengagement talks, Kissinger confirmed Sadat's assessment that only the U.S., with close ties to Israel, could bring about a satisfactory Middle East settlement. Kissinger's adroit diplomacy not only limited Soviet influence, but also set the stage for the Camp David peace process in the late 1970s.

Henry Kissinger served as National Security Adviser and later as Secretary of State in the administrations of Presidents Richard Nixon and Gerald Ford.

CHAPTER 2

The Military Arrives

From Jimmy Carter to George W. Bush

Jimmy Carter, having come into office determined to forge a comprehensive peace agreement in the Middle East, was faced with a number of circumstances and events not of his making and over which he had little control—events that led to the beginning of more direct U.S. military intervention. Although the U.S. and Israel had been facilitating the rise of **Hamas** as a counterbalance to **Fatah** and the PLO, by the mid-1970s the PLO, under Yasser Arafat, had become the dominant voice of Palestinian nationalism. Carter tried to organize a multinational conference that, although not including the PLO, would include Palestinian representatives. However, given strong opposition from Israel and splits within his own administration, Carter was forced to abandon the conference proposal.

Faced with the failure of the multinational conference, Egypt's **Anwar Sadat** decided on a bilateral approach. Two principles had informed Arab diplomacy since the 1967 War:

1. There could be no negotiations with Israel until Israel withdrew from all territories occupied in 1967.

Hamas is the Palestinian Sunni-Islamic organization with an associated military wing, located in the Palestinian territories.

Fatah is a leading Palestinian political party and the largest faction of the confederated multi-party Palestine Liberation Organization (PLO).

Anwar Sadat was the third President of Egypt, serving from October 15, 1970, until his assassination on October 6, 1981.

19

2. Any such negotiations would be conducted by the Arab states collectively.

Menachem Begin was an Israeli politician, founder of Likud and the sixth Prime Minister of the State of Israel. He died in 1992.

As a result of this policy, all Arab nations and the PLO opposed Sadat's initiative. In 1978, Carter invited Sadat and Israeli Prime Minister **Menachem Begin** to Camp David for bilateral talks mediated by Carter himself. Sadat came to Camp David with the objective of recovering all Arab lands occupied in 1967. He knew if he failed in this effort, he would be seen as a traitor to the Arab cause. Sadat ended up agreeing to a peace treaty that normalized diplomatic relations with Israel in return for Israel's withdrawal from the Sinai. There was also a vague agreement on a transitional authority to replace the Israeli occupation forces and for Israel to cease settlement building on the West Bank. The language was such that each side could interpret the agreement in terms that best suited their particular view. In the end Begin denied that he had made any such agreement and continued the settlement building. The whole agreement was widely denounced in the Arab world and in 1981 Sadat was assassinated. However, a cold peace between Israel and Egypt has endured.

The **Camp David Accords** were a peace treaty between Israel and Egypt resulting from talks at Camp David between Egyptian President Sadat, Israeli Prime Minister Begin, and the host, U.S. President Carter. They were signed in 1979.

The ink was not even dry on the much-acclaimed **Camp David Accords** when President Carter was thrown into the turmoil of the Iranian Revolution and the Iran Hostage Crisis. Although Carter, during his election campaign, had pledged to support human rights around the world, once elected, he felt that Iran was so strategically important that he had to ignore the shah's atrocious human rights record. His political and moral support for the shah outraged ordinary Iranians.

Beginning in early 1978 massive anti-government demonstrations swept Iran. Carter's administration was deeply divided over how the U.S. should respond. Secretary of State,

Cyrus Vance, felt that supporting the shah was futile and that the U.S. should encourage him to relinquish some or all of his power. On the other hand, National Security Adviser, Zbigniew Brzezinski, a Cold War hawk, felt that the shah, an important American ally, could hold on if he launched an even more massive crackdown. As Washington dithered, events overtook them and, on January 16, 1979, the shah and the empress fled the country.

On February 1, 1979, **Ayatollah Ruhollah Khomeini,** a figure who had been exiled by the shah and who was little known prior to the start of the uprising, returned in triumph as the leader of the revolution. In early 1979, it was unclear what kind of a government would succeed the shah. A variety of political groups, secular and Islamist, communist and socialist and everything in between vied for power. Carter felt that there was some possibility of establishing relations with a more tolerable government than an Islamist govern-

Ayatollah Ruhollah Khomeini was the supreme religious leader of the Islamic Republic of Iran in 1979, and after successfully removing Shah Pahlavi from power, was named religious and political leader of Iran for life. He died in 1989.

ment led by Khomeini. To that end he increased embassy staffing and the CIA established contacts with more secular government ministers including the French-educated Abul Hassan Bani Sadr.

Americans Taken Hostage

In the fall of 1979, President Carter made a major political blunder. Carter, a devout evangelical Christian, allowed his Christian informed sense of compassion to override realist political calculations and permitted the ailing shah to enter the U.S. for cancer treatment. For the Iranians, this was a replay of 1953 when, after the shah had been ousted, the CIA orchestrated a coup and the shah was returned to power. Iranian students were convinced that the CIA was using the embassy as a staging ground for another coup and seized the building. While the embassy was under siege, embassy staff shredded many sensitive documents. The Iranians, however, were able to employ skilled Iranian carpet weavers to piece the documents back together. By 1980 the documents clearly showed the contacts by CIA agent Vernon Cassin, who passed himself off as Guy Rutherford, an American businessman, with then President, Bani Sadr. Although Bani Sadr probably didn't know that his contact was CIA, he was thoroughly discredited and forced to resign. After brutally purging his opposition, Khomeini's Islamist government was firmly in place.

The detention of the embassy staff as hostages lingered into 1980. Faced with an oil crisis caused by the Iranian disruptions, rising inflation and the challenge of the Soviet invasion of Afghanistan, President Carter was under enormous domestic political pressure to "do something." In response Carter authorized the U.S. military to undertake a complicated and risky operation to rescue the hostages. The operation was a debacle and resulted in the deaths of eight American servicemen.

Carter was desperate to obtain the release of the hostages and spent the last months of his administration trying to negotiate a deal with the Iranians. The outbreak of the Iran-Iraq War was taxing Iran's resources and the Iranians became more flexible. The Carter administration worked out a deal in which the hostages would be released in return for the U.S. release of $8 billion of frozen Iranian assets and a U.S. pledge not to interfere in internal Iranian affairs. In one final "thumb-in-the-eye" to Carter, the Iranians refused to release the hostages while Carter was president and only did so once Ronald Reagan was inaugurated. Just as the 1953 coup frames the Iranian view of the U.S., this episode, more than any other, frames the American view of Iran.

Rise of the Mujahideen

In the 1980s the U.S. waged a successful proxy war against the Soviet Union in Afghanistan. In the process, the U.S. unleashed forces that would culminate in events which, following the 9/11 attacks, Ambassador Ed Peck would describe as "America's chickens coming home to roost."

The Soviet Union, with its long border with Afghanistan, had long had a strong interest in and wielded a large influence in Afghanistan. The long border abutted the Soviet republics, which are now modern day Turkmenistan, Uzbekistan and Tajikistan. These republics contain restive Muslim populations with strong ethnic and tribal ties across the border in Afghanistan. In 1978, a pro-Soviet government came to power in Afghanistan, which gave rise to an Islamic rebel group called the *Mujahideen*. Concerned that the Soviet Union would use Afghanistan as an entry point to threaten the Persian Gulf and seeing an opportunity to give the Soviets a bloody nose, Zbigniew Brzezinski convinced President Carter to begin sending covert aid to the *Mujahideen*. The Soviets, disturbed about the effect that an Islamic state in Afghanistan would have on the Muslim populations in their bordering republics, were equally determined to prevent Afghanistan from going Islamic. In 1979, the Soviets became convinced that the government in Kabul was unable or unwilling to crush the *Mujahideen*.

> *Mujahideen—* Literally in Arabic means "those who struggle in the path of Allah." In Western parlance it has come to refet to radical Islamic fighers

On December 25, 1979, the Soviet Union launched a massive invasion of Afghanistan. President Carter, seeing the Soviet action as a serious threat to American security, responded by promulgating what became known as the Carter Doctrine. The doctrine promised "an attempt by outside forces to gain control of the Persian Gulf region will be repelled by any means necessary, including military force." Carter also stepped up support for the *Mujahideen*.

Charlie Wilson's War

Under the Reagan administration aid to the *Mujahideen* increased dramatically and thus began Operation Cyclone, or what became known in popular culture as "Charlie Wilson's War." Aided by Saudi Arabia, the U.S. recruited tens of thousands of young Muslim men in the Middle East and North Africa to join the *jihad* in Afghanistan against "the godless Communists." The aid effort was mainly funneled through the Pakistani government of Muhammad Zia-ul-Haq. Zia-ul-Haq, a conservative Muslim who supported an Islamic state in Pakistan and Afghanistan, was more than willing to help. In return for this help, the Reagan administration turned a blind eye to Zia-ul-Haq's human rights abuses and nuclear weapons program.

When the U.S. began to supply the *Mujahideen* with Stinger

Taliban is an Islamic fundamentalist political movement in Afghanistan and has been led by spiritual leader Mohammed Omar since 1994.

Omar Abdel-Rahman, commonly known in the United States as "The Blind Sheikh," is currently serving a life sentence in a U.S. prison. His prosecution grew out of investigations of his involvement in the planning of the 1993 World Trade Center bombings.

Osama bin Laden was the founder of al-Qaeda, the Sunni militant Islamist organization that claimed responsibility for the September 11 attacks on the United States, along with numerous other mass casualty attacks against civilian and military targets. He was killed in Pakistan on May 2, 2011.

shoulder fired anti-aircraft missiles capable of shooting down Soviet helicopters, the tide of the war began to shift in favor of the rebels. By 1987, Soviet President Mikhail Gorbachev had concluded that the Soviet Union could no longer afford the financial, human and political cost of its Afghan campaign and began to withdraw Soviet troops. The Soviet military was gone by 1989 leaving behind the puppet government of Mohammad Najibullah in Kabul. Having defeated the Soviet Union, the U.S. lost all interest in Afghanistan and withdrew its personnel and stopped all support. The Najibullah regime collapsed in 1992 and factions in the *Mujahideen* quickly began to fight among themselves. These factions were variously supported by Saudi Arabia, Iran and Pakistan. After several years of chaos and bloody civil war, the **Taliban**, strongly supported by Pakistan, gained control of most of Afghanistan in 1996. The Taliban brought a semblance of order to the country and imposed a strict and extremely austere version of Islamic law.

Among the young men recruited by the CIA to support and fight with the *Mujahideen* in Afghanistan were a blind Egyptian Cleric **Sheikh Omar Abdel-Rahman** and **Osama bin Laden**, a wealthy Saudi of Yemeni extraction. These men will be heard from again in a few years for their unsuccessful and successful efforts to bomb the World Trade Center. After defeating the godless Communists, it wasn't a big stretch for them to convince their fellow jihadists to defeat the godless Americans.

The Reagan administration's Middle East policies were greatly informed by his worldview that the Soviet Union, the evil empire, was the root of all the problems in the world. He strongly embraced Israel as a staunch ally against Soviet expansionism. He also assumed that Syria was a proxy of the Soviet Union and sought to contain it and he clashed with Libya's Muammar Gaddafi, who received Soviet economic and military aid. That said, much of Reagan's Middle East efforts were directed at containing non-state actors such as Hezbollah.

The Israeli Invasion of Lebanon

In 1982 Israel invaded Lebanon with the stated intent of destroying the PLO, who had reestablished its base in Beirut after being evicted from Jordan. The Reagan administration initially gave tacit approval to the Israeli invasion. However, once Israel began to bombard Beirut, Reagan dispatched an envoy to broker a ceasefire. Under the ceasefire agreement, the PLO agreed to decamp to Tunisia, while Israel agreed to withdraw from Lebanon. As the PLO departed, thousands of Palestinian refugees were left behind in refugee camps throughout Lebanon. Following the assassination of Lebanese President-elect Bachir Gemayel, a Christian warlord supported by Israel, Christian militias, aided by the Israeli Army under the command of Ariel Sharon, attacked the refugee camps of Sabra and Shatila and massacred hundreds of civilians including many women and children. (This event would return to haunt Israeli-Palestinian relations in 2000.) In order to prevent further atrocities, the Reagan administration dispatched the U.S. Marines to Lebanon.

> *Hezbollah* is a Shia Islamic militant group and political party based in Lebanon.

Since the 1979 Iranian revolution, Iran had seen itself as the protector of minority Shia populations around the Middle East. When Israel invaded Lebanon, representatives of **Hezbollah** (at the time a mainly social service group supporting Shia communities in Lebanon) were in Tehran for a conference. They asked Iran for support in an effort to resist the Israeli invasion. Iran readily agreed. Hezbollah proved to be a very effective adversary. The group attacked and harassed Israeli forces and the Marines, whom they saw as protectors of Israel. In October 1983, suicide bombers blew up the U.S. Marine barracks in Beirut, killing 241 American soldiers prompting Reagan, in February 1984, to begin the withdrawal of the remaining Marines.

This episode was not the end of the U.S.'s Lebanese troubles. Many Americans lived in Beirut, the "Paris of the East," and were targets of hostage takers, primarily from Hezbollah. Under great political pressure to obtain the release of various hostages, the administration began what evolved into the bizarre "arms for hostages" deal with Iran. Using Israel as an intermediary, the U.S. agreed to sell arms to Iran and in return Iran would use its influence with Hezbollah to obtain the release of some of the hostages. To add to the debacle of negotiating with Iran, America's sworn enemy, someone in the administration came up with an idea to get around congressional restrictions on aid to the "Contra" rebels in Nicaragua. In what came to be known as the **"Iran-Contra Affair,"** profits from the arms sales to Iran were diverted to the "Contras." For the Reagan administration the political fallout of this convoluted policy was enormous.

Iran-Contra Affair was a political scandal in the United States that came to light in November 1986. During the Reagan administration, senior administration officials secretly facilitated the sale of arms to Iran, the subject of an arms embargo. Some U.S. officials also hoped that the arms sales would secure the release of several hostages and allow U.S. intelligence agencies to fund the Nicaraguan Contras.

Try as he might to focus foreign policy attention on the Soviet Union, Reagan could not avoid issues in the Middle East. In December 1987, Palestinians living on the West Bank and Gaza began what is now called the First *Intifada* or uprising. For 20 years Palestinians had been living under Israeli military occupation, which controlled every aspect of their lives. Finally frustrated with the status quo, which seemed to have no end in sight, and the ongoing Israeli settlement building, the Palestinians began largely peaceful protests, including refusal to pay taxes, economic boycotts, popular demonstrations, road barricading, etc. The Israeli military responded with a policy of "breaking Palestinian bones" and deployed 80,000 troops in Gaza and the West Bank to quell the uprising. As the violence escalated on both sides, over 1,000 people were killed.

Palestinians and PLO Gain Favor

The international community viewed the Israeli response to what was consciously a non-violent protest movement as disproportionate and cruel and harshly criticized Israel's actions. In contrast, however, Palestinians and the PLO began to be seen more favorably. As the U.S. media began to openly criticize Israel, the U.S. felt pressure to engage with the PLO. Unwilling to deal directly with the PLO, Secretary of State George Shultz tried to have the Palestinians represented in bilateral talks as part of a joint Jordanian/Palestinian delegation. Jordan trumped this strategy by relinquishing all claims to the West Bank. Even after much diplomatic maneuvering, the U.S. was forced to recognize the PLO as the Palestinian representative at the bilateral talks, even though little came out of Israeli/Palestinian meetings. The *intifada* did, however, raise the profile of the Palestinian cause and international criticism of Israel's policies in the occupied territories became more open.

The Iran-Iraq War

In order to understand the policies of the George H. W. Bush administration and the First Gulf War, a little historical context is necessary, in particular regarding the Iran-Iraq War of the 1980s. Following the upheaval of the Iranian revolution, Iraq's President **Saddam Hussein** saw an opportunity to

Saddam Hussein was the fifth President of Iraq, serving in this capacity from July 16, 1979, until April 9, 2003. In 2003, a coalition led by the U.S. and U.K. invaded Iraq to depose Saddam, after accusing him of possessing weapons of mass destruction and having ties to al-Qaeda. Following his capture on December 13, 2003, he was tried and convicted of charges related to the 1982 killing of 148 Iraqi Shiites and was sentenced to death by hanging. His execution was carried out on December 30, 2006.

weaken his Shia rival Iran and annex oil rich Khuzestan Province in western Iran. In September 1980, Iraq launched a surprise attack on Iran. Although Iraq had some initial limited success, Iran soon went on the offensive and quickly regained its lost territories and invaded Basra province in Iraq. For the next eight years Iran remained on the offensive. Although officially neutral, the Reagan administration, concerned about an Iranian "march to Jerusalem," saw Iraq as the lesser of two evils. The U.S. and its allies provided aid to the Iraqi war effort in the form of financial credits, intelligence information on Iranian military strength and positioning, and weapons (including chemical weapons) technology.

In what is known as the "Tanker War," Iran and Iraq declared and enforced blockades of oil shipments from the other ports, disrupting the flow of oil through the Strait of Hormuz. In 1984, responding to the threat to oil supplies, the U.S. began reflagging neutral tankers and escorting these tankers in convoys through the strait. This strategy brought U.S. military forces into direct confrontation with Iranian and Iraqi forces, resulting in the destruction of planes and ships and causing casualties on all sides. In 1988, the confrontation culminated with the shooting down by the USS Vincennes of Iran Air Flight 655 bound from Bandar Abbas to Dubai resulting in the deaths of 290 civilians. After eight bloody years of war, which claimed over one million lives on both sides, (many as a result of Iraqi chemical attacks on Iranian cities), the conflict ended in a stalemate.

Shortly after the end of the Iran-Iraq War, disputes arose between Iraq and Kuwait over issues such as Kuwait's refusal to forgive Iraqi debt incurred fighting the war, Iraqi territorial claims on Kuwait, dating from the Ottoman Empire, Kuwait's overproducing its OPEC quotas in an effort to recover revenues lost during the war and Kuwait's alleged slant drilling into Iraqi territory. As the disputes escalated, in July 1990 Iraq massed thousands of troops on the Kuwait border. Negotiations to end the crisis broke down and, on August 2, 1990, Iraq launched an invasion of Kuwait. After a brief conflict, Saddam Hussein announced the annexation of Kuwait, giving him control of 20 percent of the world's oil. Iraq also appeared to threaten Saudi Arabia, which contained another 20 percent. In response, President Bush took a forceful position saying that such naked aggression "could not stand."

Operation Desert Storm

Working closely with the U.N. Security Council, the Bush administration was able to pass a resolution condemning the invasion and demanding immediate Iraqi withdrawal from Kuwait. Although a number of the justifications used by the administration for intervention later turned out to be false George Bush was able to assemble a military and financial coalition of 36 nations to support military action against Iraq. Despite a massive $11 million public relations campaign by the Kuwaiti government in support of the war, the congressional war resolution passed by relatively modest margins of only 52-47 in the Senate and 250-181 in the house. These margins, along with large anti-war demonstrations, reflected the unease within the American public about getting involved in a Middle East war. Despite last minute efforts by Saddam to achieve a diplomatic solution, on January 17, 1991, the coalition launched "Operation Desert Storm" with air attacks. On February 23, coalition forces launched a ground offensive to expel Iraqi forces from Kuwait. On February 27 President Bush announced the liberation of Kuwait.

Since the Iraqi Army was in complete disarray, it is likely that coalition forces could have advanced to Baghdad and overthrown Saddam Hussein. Bush, however, wary of the tenuous political situation at home and conscious of the limited nature of the U.N. resolution, declined to do so. Bush did, however, encourage the Iraqi people to overthrow Saddam Hussein, leaving the impression that he would intervene to aid such a rebellion. When the Kurds in the north and the Shia in the south attempted such a rebellion, Bush had second thoughts and, despite some criticism, declined to intervene. Left to his own devices, Saddam brutally crushed the rebellions. In reaction to this brutality, the U.S. established "no-fly zones" in the north and the south that remained in place until the Second Gulf War in 2003. The reaction of the Iraqi people to the 2003 American invasion was heavily influenced by the perceived betrayal by the Americans of their 1991 revolution.

The Negotiation of the Oslo Accords

In 1991, in Oslo, Norway, the Israelis and the PLO began negotiating in complete secrecy with little outside involvement. In the so-called Oslo Accords, signed in 1993, the parties agreed that Israel would withdraw from portions of the occupied territories and that the Palestinians would form a self-governing authority (Palestinian Authority or PA) that would administer unspecified portions of the occupied territories. Seeing this agreement as a breakthrough, President Clinton, ever the politician, brought the parties to Washington for a Rose Garden signing ceremony.

The agreement was seen as a five-year transitional document leading to a final status agreement no later than 1998. The Accords were much ballyhooed around the globe with Yasser Arafat, Shimon Peres and Yitzhak Rabin receiving the 1994 Nobel Peace Prize. The agreement was flawed, however, since all of the difficult issues (borders, status of Jerusalem, status of refugees and the fate of Jewish settlements in the occupied territories) were deferred until final status talks.

Rejectionists on both sides, primarily religious fundamentalists, tried to derail the process. In November 1994, a right wing Jew massacred 29 Palestinians at the Cave of the Patriarchs in Hebron and in November 1995, another right wing Jew assassinated Yitzhak Rabin. Also in the mid 1990's, Hamas initiated a campaign of terrorist attacks within Israel that killed dozens of Israeli civilians. During the so called "Oslo Years," the settler population on the West Bank increased by over 100,000 and by 2000, Israel had withdrawn from only 40 percent of the territory.

In July 2000, President Clinton convened a summit meeting between Yasser Arafat and Ehud Barak at Camp David. Arafat was reluctant to attend as there was little consensus in the PA about what an agreement should look like and many felt that the summit was premature. Despite these misgivings, Arafat agreed to attend. Because no written record of the proceedings was kept, exactly what transpired is unclear.

After two weeks of negotiations, it appears Ehud Barak offered to withdraw from 91 percent of the West Bank and Gaza. However, because of settlements and bypass roads, the resulting Palestinian state would have been broken up into separate enclaves. Israel also insisted on retaining control of Jerusalem. Realizing that it was not possible for him to sell such an agreement to the PA, Arafat rejected the plan and flew home. President Clinton endorsed Barak's proposal and blamed the failure of the talks on Arafat.

The Second *Intifada*

In September 2000, **Ariel Sharon**, a notorious figure among Palestinians for his role in the 1982 Sabra and Shatila massacres in Lebanon, took a walk through the al-Aqsa Mosque in the Haram al-Sharif (The Noble Sanctuary), the third holiest site in Islam. The Jews know the site as the Temple Mount, the site of Herod's Temple that was destroyed in 70 CE. Because of concerns by Muslims that Israel will destroy the Muslim holy sites in order to rebuild the temple, this event helped spark the Second *Intifada*. The

Ariel Sharon was an Israeli politician and general who served as the 11th Prime Minister of Israel until he was incapacitated by a stroke. Sharon was a commander in the Israeli Army from its creation in 1948.

Second *Intifada* was much different from the First *Intifada*. It was not a popular uprising, but was instigated by Palestinian leadership. It also was much more violent. A campaign of terrorist bombings within Israel had the effect of hardening Israeli political opinion.

In February 2001, a right wing government under Ariel Sharon was elected and the situation went from bad to terrible. Sharon tightened control over the occupied territories and stepped up the targeted assassinations of militants. In turn the militants stepped up their suicide bombings. Over the period of the Second *Intifada* (2000-2005) over 3,000 Palestinians were killed and over 1,000 Israelis, military and civilian, were killed. As the world was watching this unfold in Israel-Palestine, on September 11, 2001 an event occurred which would dramatically affect U.S. Middle East policy.

The Terrorist Attacks of 9/11

The terrorist attacks of September 11, 2001 were a shock to the government, the American people and to George W. Bush personally.

During his campaign for the presidency in 2000, Bush had stressed a more "humble" foreign policy saying, "If we're an arrogant nation, they'll resent us. If we're a humble nation, but strong, they'll welcome us." Traumatized by the level of physical, human and economic damage wrought by the terrorists, Bush immediately declared a set of policy principles that became known as the Bush Doctrine. These principles, as he described them in his 2010 memoir, were:

1. Make no distinction between terrorists and the nations that harbor them—and hold both to account.

2. Take the fight to the enemy overseas before they can attack us again here at home.

3. Confront threats before they fully materialize.

4. Advance liberty and hope as an alternative to the enemy's ideology of repression and fear[5].

U.S. Launches Operation Enduring Freedom

Al-Qaeda (literally in Arabic "the Base") is a global militant Islamist and takfiri organization founded by Abdullah Yusuf Azzam and Osama bin Laden in Peshawar, Pakistan in 1988/89 to coordinate manning and financing of the Mujahideen fighting the Soviet Union in Afghanistan.

The practical implications of this policy were first manifested in late 2001 in Afghanistan with its Taliban-led government. The Bush administration demanded that the Taliban government turn over Osama bin Laden, whom they suspected of being behind the 9/11 attacks. The Taliban refused to turn bin Laden over without seeing proof of his involvement. The U.S. refused to negotiate and on October 7, 2001 launched "Operation Enduring Freedom." This operation, initially, was primarily a Special Forces operation. With the assistance of Iran, the so-called Northern Alliance, an anti-Taliban organization opposed to the Taliban-led Islamic Emirate, was given ammunition and supplies and persuaded to join the effort.

Using Northern Alliance intelligence and American air power, the Special Forces, many embedded with Northern Alliance forces, quickly ousted the Taliban and **al-Qaeda** from their strongholds.

Unfortunately, as a result of the limited number of forces deployed, bin Laden was not captured and he and his al-Qaeda associates escaped into Pakistan. In December 2001, at a conference in Bonn, Germany, the U.S., again with the assistance of Iran, orchestrated the selection of Hamid Karzai as the new leader of Afghanistan. As the mission in Afghanistan became one of "nation building," the Bush administration focused the attention of the "War on Terror" elsewhere.

Bush Names "Axis of Evil" Countries

The first sign that the "War on Terror" was expanding beyond the boundaries of enemies tied to the 9/11 attacks came in Bush's January 2002 State of the Union address when he identified Iraq, Iran and North Korea as part of an "Axis of Evil" that threatened the United States. The inclusion of Iran in this axis, despite its assistance in overthrowing the Taliban, has helped persuade Iranian leadership that there is nothing they can do to improve relations with the U.S.

Shortly after the 9/11 attacks, Secretary of Defense Donald Rumsfeld ordered his aides to look for evidence of Iraq's involvement in the attacks. With the evidence of Iraqi involvement flimsy at best, the Bush administration turned its attention to Iraq's alleged weapons of mass destruction (WMD). This led to the formalization of a policy of unilateral preventative military action against countries believed to be developing WMD.

On March 20, 2003, the U.S. and its allies launched an invasion of Iraq, which led to the overthrow of Saddam Hussein's government and a U.S. occupation of Iraq. The repercussions from these actions would impact events throughout the Middle East for the next decade.

CHAPTER 3

The Fall of the Post WWI Middle East

From George W. Bush to Barack Obama

The 2003 invasion of Iraq by the U.S. and its partners in the "coalition of the willing" began a series of events and a process of political upheaval that drastically changed the geopolitical landscape of the Middle East region. The initial invasion, which began on March 20, 2003, was a quick and decisive operation. On April 9, Baghdad fell to the coalition forces, ending the 24-year reign of Saddam Hussein and the Ba'ath party. The fall of Saddam Hussein's brutal regime was initially greeted with an outpouring of euphoria that was stage managed by the coalition authorities to build support for the invasion.[6]

The initial euphoria quickly deteriorated into civil unrest including looting of government buildings, museums and cultural centers as well as increasing crime. The beginning signs of the upcoming insurgency began to appear as anti-U.S. groups made their presence felt through demonstrations and protests.[7]

Immediately after the fall of Saddam Hussein, the invading coalition established the Coalition Provisional Authority (CPA) as the interim government of Iraq. Having given little thought about or planning for the day after, the Bush administration appeared to be creating a plan on the fly. The first head of the CPA was Ret. General Jay Garner. On May 11, 2003, he was replaced by Paul Bremer, a retired Foreign Service officer and consultant. Immediately upon assuming the position, Bremer made two decisions that would change the course of events in Iraq and neighboring countries for over a decade. On May 23, 2003, Bremer issued Order Number 2, which dismantled the Iraqi Army thereby putting over 400,000 trained Iraqi soldiers out of work, creating a security vacuum and providing a ready source of fighters in what would soon become an Iraqi insurgency. Shortly thereafter, Bremer announced a "de-Ba'athfication policy," which banned any member of the ruling Ba'ath party from holding any position in the new Iraqi government. These bureaucrats were the ones who knew how to run the government and thus the new government, lacking effective leadership and management, was hamstrung from the beginning. Following the capture of Saddam Hussein in December 2003, insurgent elements began to appear opposing both the CPA and its appointed interim Iraqi government.

The Insurgency Expands

In the spring of 2004, with the arrival on the scene of well-organized insurgent groups such as al-Qaeda in Iraq (led by Abu Musab al-Zarqawi) and the Shia Mahdi Army, the insurgency against coalition forces and the interim government began to expand. Coalition attempts to suppress the insurgency led to the First and Second Battles of Fallujah, which resulted in the destruction of the city creating many thousands of internally displaced Sunni citizens. Following the 2005 election of the transitional Iraqi government, a government dominated by Shia politicians, al-Qaeda in Iraq, strengthened by the addition of many disgruntled Sunni Iraqis as well as foreign fighters from Syria and Saudi Arabia, initiated a strategy of fomenting a sectarian civil war. Al-Qaeda suicide bombings, targeting Shia holy sites and civilian gatherings, killed hundreds of Shia civilians. Despite the ongoing violence Iraq managed to ratify a constitution and elect a National Assembly. It appeared that the U.S. experiment of imposing democracy in the Middle East by force might actually succeed. President Bush was confident enough in success to proclaim in his 2005 inaugural address that "…it is the policy of the United States to seek and support the growth of democratic movements and institutions in every nation and culture, with the ultimate goal of ending tyranny in our world."[8]

2006 Gaza and Lebanon Wars

Palestinian Authority (PA) Legislative Council elections were scheduled for January 25, 2006. Members of the ruling Fatah party, as well as leaders of Israel, concerned that Hamas, the militant Islamist group, considered a terrorist organization by the U.S. and Israel, would do well in the election, advised Palestinian President, Mahmoud Abbas to postpone the elections. Under pressure by U.S. democracy advocates, Abbas decided to go ahead with the elections. The result was a landslide victory for Hamas. Despite winning only 44 percent of the popular vote, Hamas won 74 of 132 legislative seats and on March 29 the Hamas government was sworn in. The U.S. and EU immediately cut off aid, severed all contact with the PA and began to arm and train Fatah forces to oppose Hamas.

In the midst of ongoing conflict between Fatah and Hamas forces, Israel, responding to a cross border raid from Gaza, which resulted in the death of two Israeli soldiers and the capture of another, attacked Gaza. This resulted in a five-month war between Israel and Hamas forces in Gaza. Throughout the war and even after the ceasefire, conflict continued between Hamas and Fatah. Eventually, in June 2007, Fatah forces were expelled from Gaza and the Palestinian territories were divided into two separate entities, the West Bank and Gaza.

In July 2006, Lebanese Hezbollah militia forces conducted a cross border raid into Israel that resulted in the death of eight Israeli soldiers and the capture of two others. According to Hezbollah leader Hassan Nasrallah, the goal of the incursion was to capture Israeli soldiers as hostages for a prisoner exchange for Palestinians held by Israel.[9] Instead of negotiating a prisoner exchange, Israel attacked Lebanon in an effort to weaken Hezbollah and destroy its military capability. Following an inconclusive 34-day war, which killed 1,100 Lebanese, mostly civilians, and 132 Israelis, mostly soldiers, Israeli forces withdrew from Lebanon. During this carnage, U.S. Secretary of State, Condoleezza Rice, famously dismissed the death and destruction as "the birth pangs of the new Middle East."[10] Eventually, in July 2008, the bodies of the two captured Israeli soldiers were exchanged for five Palestinian prisoners and four Hezbollah fighters captured during the war. Israel also returned the bodies of 200 fighters whose bodies had been brought to Israel.

The Iraqi Civil War and the U.S. Troop Surge

In May 2006, a permanent Iraqi government, headed by Shia politician Nouri al-Maliki, took power. As conditions on the ground in Iraq continued to worsen and following a damning report by the Iraq Study Group that declared, "the situation in Iraq is grave and deteriorating,"[11] the Bush administration deployed 20,000 more troops to Iraq and appointed General David Petraeus to succeed General George Casey as commander of forces in Iraq. In conjunction with the "surge" of U.S. troops, General Petraeus focused the military effort on securing the population and expanding the role of Sunni tribal militias, often called "Sons of Iraq." He planned on integrating the tribal militias into the Iraqi Army. This integration of the Sunnis into the Army was never implemented by Shia Prime Minister Maliki, adding to a sectarian divide that would come back to haunt Iraq in the future. As violence decreased, political leaders in Iraq and the U.S. began to plan for a drawdown of coalition forces. Many U.S. allies had already begun to withdraw their forces and, in December 2008, the U.S. and Iraq signed a Status of Forces Agreement that provided that the U.S. would withdraw from Iraqi cities by June 30, 2009 and that all U.S. forces would be out of Iraq by December 31, 2011.

Operation Cast Lead

On December 27, 2008, citing a need to suppress rocket fire from the Gaza Strip into Israel and a need to stop weapons smuggling into the Gaza Strip, Israel attacked the Gaza enclave in a military operation dubbed "Operation Cast Lead." The operation continued for three weeks until, faced with increasing casualties and rising international criticism, Israel declared a unilateral ceasefire on January 18, 2009. The conflict resulted in 1,400 Palestinian deaths, mostly civilians and 13 Israeli deaths, mostly military. As was the case in previous Israel-Gaza conflicts, the ceasefire resolved none of the underlying causes. Rocket fire gradually resumed, the blockade of Gaza remained in place, preventing reconstruction of destroyed buildings and infrastructure, and the resulting poverty and hopelessness continued to breed militant resistance.

Withdrawal of U.S. Forces from Iraq

In January 2009, attributing the decline in violence in Iraq to the troop surge, the growth of the Awakening Councils or Sons of Iraq and Shia leader Muqtada al-Sadr's decision to abide by a ceasefire, the Obama administration, in accordance with the terms of the Status of Forces agreement negotiated by the Bush administration, began to draw down U.S. military forces. In February, President Obama announced that the U.S. combat mission in Iraq would end by August 2010. On the political front things were not going as well. Provincial elections were marred by violence, assassination threats, complaints of fraud and a relatively low voter turnout. In April, tens of thousands of Iraqis rallied in major cities, demanding an immediate withdrawal of coalition forces. Reflecting the change of mission from combat to support, Operation Iraqi Freedom was renamed, "Operation New Dawn." Despite counter terrorism operations that resulted in the deaths of a number of senior al-Qaeda leaders, sectarian and anti-coalition violence continued unabated. As sectarian political gridlock continued in Baghdad, a number of members of the Awakening Councils began to defect to insurgent groups or to al-Qaeda in Iraq, setting the stage for future unrest. With violence continuing and Iraqi forces appearing unable to cope with it, the Obama administration attempted to renegotiate the Bush era Status of Forces agreement to allow the continued presence of U.S. forces in Iraq after the December 31, 2011 deadline. The Iraqi government, however, insisted that any residual American forces would not have immunity and would be subject to prosecution under Iraqi law. This condition has long been unsatisfactory to American officials and thus the last American forces withdrew from Iraq on December 18, 2011, ending one of the most controversial military undertakings in American history. The last American soldier to die in Iraq before the withdrawal, was killed by a roadside bomb on November 14, 2011.

The Arab Spring

The Arab Spring or Arab Awakening describes a wave of demonstrations, riots and political unrest that spread across the Middle East and

North Africa (MENA) beginning in Tunisia in December 2010. These events drove a number of government regimes from power, caused numerous political upheavals and led to civil conflicts in many of the countries involved. The stage for this tectonic shift in the MENA was set by the confluence of factors including large young unemployed populations, economic stagnation, the inability of entrenched autocratic regimes to address the issues, wealth inequality and large-scale corruption. Most observers of the region recognized that the situation in these countries was at best unstable, but almost no one saw the changes coming in the manner that they did. On December 17, 2010, Mohamed Bouazizi, a 27-year-old street vendor in Sidi Bouzid, a small city in central Tunisia, set himself on fire in protest of the confiscation of his wares and the harassment and humiliation that was inflicted on him. The demonstrations inspired by this event spread like a wildfire across MENA.

Tunisia

Triggered by the self-emulation by Bouazizi, the massive street demonstrations that followed this event were protesting high unemployment, food inflation, corruption and generally poor living conditions under the authoritarian regime of longtime President Zine El Abidine Ben Ali. The demonstrations began on December 17, 2010, and on January 14, 2011 Ben Ali resigned and left the country. A caretaker government was established that included opposition leaders as well as members of Ben Ali's party (CDR). Protests continued until all members of the CDR were expelled from the government. On October 23, 2011, elections were held in which the Islamist party, Ennahda, won a plurality of the seats in Parliament. Although Islamist in character, the Ennahda party has retained the secular nature of the Tunisian government.

Egypt

On January 25, 2011, a series of demonstrations, marches, acts of civil disobedience, riots and strikes began calling for the ouster of President Hosni Mubarak. The protests were greeted with a brutal crackdown by Egyptian security forces. The crackdown only inflamed the unrest and attracted international condemnation. As the unrest spread across Egypt, with many areas dissolving into looting and chaos, the U.S. and its western allies were torn between having concern for the effects of a crackdown that caused numerous civilian casualties and maintaining stability in an important regional ally that had a peace treaty with Israel. On February 11, 2011, Mubarak resigned as President, the Constitution was suspended and power was transferred to a military junta, the Supreme Council of the Armed Forces (SCAF). SCAF ruled Egypt until a messy political process and a series of elections brought the Muslim Brotherhood in Egypt to power. Mohammed Morsi, leader of the Muslim Brotherhood, became President of Egypt. The rule of the Muslim Brotherhood government was chaotic, in many ways incompetent and vehemently opposed by secularists, the military and remnants of the Mubarak regime. In June, 2013, amid massive protests against the Morsi government, a group of military officers, led by General Abdel Fattah el-Sisi, staged a coup d'état that overthrew the government and returned Egypt to military rule. The U.S., relieved to see the Islamist government overthrown, and hoping that stability might return to Egypt, refused to call the coup, a coup, tacitly showing approval. The U.S. restored military aid to Egypt and in 2014 el-Sisi was elected president under a new constitution which gave more power to the president and the military and banned any religiously based political parties. This turn of events prompted many observers to call it Mubarakism, without Mubarak.

Libya

The Libyan revolution began with a series of demonstrations and uprisings against the government of Muammar Gaddafi beginning in January and February 2011. As the unrest began to morph into civil war with the formation by the rebels of a National Transitional Council (NTC), the Gaddafi government responded with increasing force. With the NTC controlling large areas of eastern Libya and establishing a government seat in Benghazi, the government forces began an offensive to reclaim lost territory. Fearing a massacre of civilians in Benghazi and seeing an opportunity to overthrow a longtime nemesis in Gaddafi, the U.S. and its allies, primarily Britain and France, pushed through a UN Security Council resolution under Article 7 of the UN Charter authorizing member states "to take all necessary measures, notwithstanding paragraph 9 of resolution 1970 (2011), to protect civilians and civilian-populated areas under threat of attack in the Libyan Arab Jamahiriya, including Benghazi, while excluding a foreign occupation force of any form on any part of Libyan territory" and "to establish a ban on all flights in the airspace of the Libyan Arab Jamahiriya in order to help protect civilians."[12] The U.S. and its coalition allies determined that the only way to protect civilians was to overthrow the Gaddafi government. The coalition began to arm rebel forces and to provide air support to these forces. In August, the Gaddafi government fell and in October Muammar Gaddafi was captured, tortured and murdered in Sirte. In the aftermath of the war, Libya descended into chaos with rival governments in Tripoli and Tobruk and vast areas that remain ungoverned and have become home for al-Qaeda and other jihadist groups. The unrest in Libya spread to Libya's neighbors, Niger, Mali, Mauretania and Algeria. In addition, the liberal interpretation of UN Security Council resolutions applied by the U.S. in this case caused Russia and China to mistrust other UN resolutions related to dealing with conflicts.

Yemen

The Yemeni Intifada (uprising) began in early 2011 with mass protests against unemployment, corruption and general economic conditions. Following months of protests, political maneuvering and violence, President Ali Abdullah Saleh resigned his position on November 23, 2011 under an agreement brokered by the Gulf Cooperation Council (GCC). On February 21, 2012, Abd Rabbuh Mansur Hadi was elected President. Modern Yemen has long been an artificial nation state made up of numerous religious, ethnic and tribal groups, which have competed for decades over economic and political advantage. No colonial or national government has been successful in bridging these differences. The new al-Hadi-led government was no exception. Despite the formation of a National Dialogue Conference intended to resolve these issues, no generally accepted solutions were forthcoming. In January

2015, the Houthis, a Zaidi (which comes from the Zaidiyyah sect of Islam) tribal group based in northern Yemen, and other allied tribal groups began a military campaign that resulted in the seizure of the capital, Sana'a, and the overthrow of the al-Hadi government. As the Houthi forces, bolstered by forces loyal to former President Saleh, advanced to control much of northern and western Yemen, Saudi Arabia and the United Arab Emirates (UAE), supported by the U.S., intervened in order to restore the al-Hadi government to power. Into the chaos created by the Civil War, al-Qaeda, in the Arabian Peninsula (AQAP), and forces allied with ISIS inserted themselves and were able to seize and control portions of southern and eastern Yemen.

Syria

In the spring of 2011, a series of protests, inspired by the Arab Spring uprisings in the Middle East and North African countries, began in Syria. The mostly peaceful demonstrations were so violently suppressed by the Assad government that the uprising gradually morphed into an armed conflict that pitted the Assad government forces, Christians, **Druze**, **Kurds** and **Alawites** supported by Iran, Russia and Hezbollah against a myriad of groups committed to overthrowing the Assad regime supported by Turkey, Saudi Arabia, the Gulf States and the U.S. These opposition forces included the secular Free Syrian Army (FSA), the Islamic State in Iraq and al-Shams (ISIS), Jabhat al-Nusra (the al-Qaeda affiliate) and a number of other Islamist groups with varying agendas. The shifting alliances among the opposition groups and the presence of outside forces created a military stalemate that has resulted in millions of internally and externally displaced refugees and a major humanitarian crisis within the

Druze are members of a political and religious sect of Islamic origin, living chiefly in Lebanon and Syria.

Kurds are an ethnic group in the Middle East.

Alawites are an Islamic sect, centered in Syria, who follow a branch of the Twelver school of Shia Islam but with syncretistic elements.

Middle East region and beyond. This flow of refugees threatened to destabilize neighboring countries.

Bahrain

The uprisings in the island state of Bahrain began in early 2011 as a protest aimed at achieving greater economic and political equality for the majority Shia population under the rule of the minority Sunni monarchy of Hamad bin Isa al-Khalifa. Following a February 17 deadly night raid by government forces on Shia neighborhoods (Bloody Thursday), the demonstrations grew and became more violent. On March 14 of that year, troops from Saudi Arabia and UAE intervened in the situation in order quell the unrest and protect the monarchy. Despite numerous efforts at reconciliation, none of the issues that created the unrest were resolved and a low level of unrest continues.

NATO Forces Begin to Withdraw from Afghanistan

In January 2013, President Obama and Afghanistan President Hamid Karzai reached an agreement that allowed for the Afghan military to assume security responsibility in Afghanistan and outlined the terms for the drawdown of U.S. forces. In the spring of 2013, this agreement was implemented and U.S. forces began to leave Afghanistan. Obama declared that "We achieved our central goal, or have come very close to achieving our central goal, which is to de-capacitate al-Qaeda, to dismantle them, to make sure that they can't attack us again," and "At the end of this conflict, we are going to be able to say that the sacrifices that were made by those men and women in uniform has (sic) brought about the goal that we sought."[13] The U.S. and Afghanistan were able to agree on a Status of Forces Agreement (SOFA) under which U.S. forces would have immunity from prosecution under the Afghan judicial system and a residual force would remain to conduct counter-terrorism operations. In October 2014, the U.S. officially ended its combat role in Afghanistan.

The Rise of ISIS

One of the unintended consequences of the invasion of Iraq was the creation of an environment that facilitated the rise of the Islamic State in Iraq and al-Sham (**ISIS**). The U.S. decision to dismantle the largely Sunni Iraqi army and to ban members of the ruling Ba'ath party from government participation created

ISIS is a Salafi jihadist militant group that follows an Islamic fundamentalist, Wahhabi doctrine of Sunni Islam.

a large pool of unemployed, disaffected, well-trained fighters who became the backbone of the insurgency against the Shia-led Iraqi government. As al-Qaeda in Iraq (AQI) became the leading force in the Sunni insurgency and fomented a sectarian conflict between Sunnis and Shia, General David Petraeus introduced a counter insurgency strategy of recruiting, bribing, and arming Sunni tribal leaders and their militias to fight against AQI. Initially, the strategy was successful, with many insurgents fleeing across the border into Syria and bringing an illusion of stability to Iraq.

As the chaos of the Syrian Civil War created large areas of ungoverned space, AQI began to reconstitute itself as ISIS and began to conquer territory within eastern Syria and western Iraq to serve as a base for operations. ISIS burst onto the international scene, when, in June 2014, it launched a coordinated attack on the major Iraqi city of Mosul, driving the Iraqi army out and threatening the capital of Baghdad. On June 29, 2014, ISIS leader Abu Bakr al-Baghdadi declared an Islamic Caliphate in the territories ruled by ISIS. These events triggered a U.S. response and, in September, President Obama announced a plan to "degrade and ultimately destroy"[14] ISIS. In order to achieve this objective, the U.S. began an aerial campaign against ISIS and began to arm and to support so-called "moderate rebels" opposed to the government of President Bashar al-Assad.

Operation Protective Edge

On July 8, 2014, in response to sporadic rocket fire from the Gaza Strip, Israel attacked Hamas-ruled Gaza in a military campaign dubbed, "Operation Protective Edge." In retaliation, Hamas began rocket attacks against Israeli infrastructure and cities. As a result of the six-week conflict, over 2,000 Gazans (mostly civilians) and over 70 Israelis (mostly military) were killed. Israel's bombing campaign completely shattered the infrastructure and housing in Gaza. Following a number of unsuccessful attempts to negotiate a ceasefire, on August 26, Hamas and Israel finally accepted a ceasefire. The war resolved none of the underlying causes of the conflict.

The EU3+3/Iran Nuclear Deal

Back in 2003, the administration under President George W. Bush began to allege that the Islamic Republic of Iran had a program to develop a nuclear weapon and started supporting dissident groups within Iran and conducting covert operations designed to disrupt the alleged program. Then, in 2006, the U.S. instituted a series of unilateral sanctions on Iranian financial institutions. During this period, the EU conducted a series of unsuccessful negotiations with Iran designed to resolve the nuclear weapons issue. Following a round of additional sanctions against Iran under the Obama administration, in 2006, Germany, France, Great Britain, Russia, China and the United States (EU3+3) began a series of negotiations to resolve the issue of Iran's nuclear program which, over the intervening years, had grown to include 20,000 uranium enrichment centrifuges and an underground enrichment site at Fordow. After several rounds of negotiations, on November 24, 2013 the parties signed an interim Joint Plan of Action (JPA), which outlined the steps to be taken to resolve the nuclear issue. In accordance with the JPA, multiple rounds of negotiations were conducted and eventually, on July 14, 2015, the involved parties signed a Joint Comprehensive Plan of Action (JCPOA). The JCPOA provides that Iran will dismantle portions of its nuclear research and enrichment program and allow for more intrusive inspections of the remaining program and in return nuclear related sanctions against Iran are to be lifted.

CHAPTER 4
Looking for the Good Guys

Americans have long had a need to be able to identify the "good guys" in any conflict situation. Maybe it's a generational thing. My generation grew up watching western movies and TV shows in which you could always tell the good guys from the bad guys. The good guys always wore white hats and the bad guys wore black. Things are far more complicated today.

At the height of the conflict in Darfur, Sudan, Brian Steidle, author of *The Devil Came on Horseback*, gave a lecture in which he tried to illuminate the complexities of this many-sided conflict. During the question and answer period, one gentleman in the audience said, "I don't understand. Who are the good guys?" Brian's answer was, "There are no good guys."

This mindset of good guys versus bad guys has carried over into the foreign policy sphere. As the U.S. has intervened in the Middle East in an effort to project power and influence on many occasions it has tried to identify reliable regional allies who would support its efforts. In many cases, finding these good guys has been mission impossible. The result has been a frequent need to invent good guys where none exist or to dub unsavory nations or groups as good guys, a strategy which has often led to disastrous consequences.

The Syrian Civil War

In the spring of 2011, inspired by other uprisings against undemocratic regimes throughout the Middle East and North Africa, large numbers of Syrians began to demonstrate against the government of

Bashar al-Assad and the Ba'ath party regime in general. The demonstrations were inspired by poor economic conditions, aggravated by a four-year-long drought, rampant corruption and human rights violations. The government responded to the peaceful demonstrators with a violent and brutal military crackdown, which in turn caused the demonstrators to take up arms. By the summer of 2011, the goals of the opposition had changed from reform of the current government to the overthrow of Assad and his entire regime. By August the opposition, augmented by defecting Syrian Army officers, had formed a governing body called the Syrian National Council with an armed wing dubbed the Free Syrian Army. As the conflict began to morph from a domestic insurgency into a full-blown civil war, outside actors began to intervene. Russia and China, fearing a repeat of the overthrow of President Muammar Gaddafi in Libya by a U.S.-led coalition under the cover of a UN resolution authorizing humanitarian assistance, refused to allow the UN to actively intervene to stop the fighting. Iran, fearing a loss of its conduit to Hezbollah in Lebanon, began to provide financial aid and military assistance to the Assad government. Hezbollah, also concerned about its Iranian connection and fearing a spillover into Lebanon, began to provide military assistance to Assad in the form of direct military intervention.

As the war continued and outside intervention increased, the opposition forces began to fragment along sectarian and ethnic lines. The Syrian National Council and the Free Syrian Army constituted the most secular of the opposition. The U.S., seeing these groups as the "good guys," began to arm, finance and train their fighters. The Islamist groups, such as the al-Qaeda affiliated Jabhat al-Nusra, Ajnad al-Sham, the Islamic Front as well as numerous small militias are supported by the Gulf Arab States, primarily Qatar and Saudi Arabia. The numerous Turkman militias are supported and armed by Turkey. The Kurdish People Protection Unit (YPG) is supported by the U.S. In this confusing mess of shifting alliances and competing groups, the Islamic State in Iraq and al-Sham (ISIS) has become the most dominant player. While not strictly a Syrian opposition group, it has managed to occupy significant territory in Syria and Iraq and declare a **caliphate**. In 2013, Secretary of State John Kerry declared that only 15-25 percent of the opposition forces are "bad guys." The problem is that this represents over 25,000 of the most dedicated, best-trained fighters and these "bad guys" are really bad.[15]

The Syrian government's Syrian Arab Army (SAA) is directly supported by Iran and the Iranian Revolutionary Guards (IRGC) Quds Force. Also supported by Iran and aligned with the government are assorted Shiite militias, Christian militias and Lebanese Hezbollah. Russia also has supported the government forces to some extent. As is frequently the case when outside actors intervene in a civil war, the conflict has deteriorated into a bloody stalemate, creating millions of refugees and thousands of casualties.

> A *caliphate* is an area ruled by a form of Islamic governance under which religious and political authority is vested in one man called the Caliph or successor to the prophet.

Early efforts to achieve a negotiated settlement were stymied by U.S. insistence that agreeing to the principle that "Assad must go" be a precondition to participation in the talks. A condition that precluded Iranian, Russian and Syrian government attendance. Infighting among opposition groups also contributed to the failed talks. As of this writing the U.S. seems to be reaching the conclusion that there are no "good guys" and that the Assad government may be the least bad alternative.

How We Got Here:

This is the first of a series of posts on my point of view on current events from a perspective gleaned from my travels to countries around the world and discussions with ordinary citizens of these countries. Hopefully, these comments will be helpful in understanding a different perspective from that which we usually receive in our mainstream media.

Assessing Options in Iraq (Blog from 8/14/2014)

Last week, President Obama, before heading to a Martha's Vineyard vacation, announced a U.S. military intervention in Iraq designed to provide humanitarian relief for the Kurdish Yazidis trapped on Mount Sinjar and to interdict an Islamic State (ISIS) military threat against the Kurdish city of Erbil. He immediately was attacked by both the left and the right for doing too much or doing too little. Republican Senators, McCain, Corker and Graham, who never met a military intervention that they didn't like, called on Obama to do more, while neglecting to mention what "more" might look like. Hillary Clinton, already in full campaign mode, criticized Obama for not arming the "moderate" Syrian opposition on the grounds that this would have prevented the rise of ISIS, a dubious assertion at best. While the core of the ISIS fighting force is relatively small (8,000-10,000), its organization and dedication has allowed it to punch well above its weight on the battlefield. Amidst all of the media hyperventilating, it might be a useful exercise to assess the policy options available to the U.S. to diffuse the crisis in Iraq.

A *takfiri* is a Sunni Muslim who accuses another Muslim (or an adherent of another Abrahamic faith) of apostasy. The accusation itself is called takfir, derived from the word kafir (unbeliever), and is described as when "one who is, or claims to be, a Muslim is declared impure."

Option One: Do nothing. Is doing nothing really an option? This option is tantamount to acceding to genocide and/or ethnic cleansing of those, such as Christians, Shias and Yazidis, in ISIS-controlled areas that are seen as apostates by the **takfiri** ISIL true believers. Beyond that humanitarian catastrophe, it would mean the breakup of Iraq as a unified state. The ISIL-controlled region would become a mecca for radical jihadists with an ambitious agenda beyond Syria and Iraq. A consolidated ISIL controlled state in the heart of the Middle East has the potential to spread the conflict to Israel, Lebanon, Jordan and beyond.

Option Two: At the other end of the spectrum is a major redeployment of American and allied troops and air power into Iraq to drive ISIL out and restore the writ of the Baghdad central government. Although Iran would probably be happy to see the U.S. again bogged down in Iraq, other local and regional players would see this major intervention as another U.S. occupation, sparking another insurgency and a return to the bad old days of 2006. It is unlikely that the American public would tolerate another war in Iraq.

Option Three: The U.S. could rely on local and/or regional players (with the most likely candidates being Iran and Turkey) to provide the boots on the ground with backing from U.S. air power. They could provide cultural knowledge, demonstrate military capability, validate strong national interest in solving the problem and establish the religious credentials to prevent this from turning into a sectarian conflict. The U.S. ability to accomplish this is uncertain at best as relations with both countries are fraught with disagreements. Iran, living with a U.S. sanctions regime, being threatened with military action, having endured assassinations and covert efforts at regime change, is in no mood to give the U.S. an easy win. Frustrated by U.S. positions in the nuclear negotiations, Iranian Supreme Leader Ali Khamenei recently said, "We will not ban them [the negotiations]. But this has become yet another invaluable experience that interaction and talks with Americans have absolutely no effect in easing their animosity [towards Iran]," "Now the events of the past year have proved this hunch to be true. Not only did we gain nothing out of these interactions, but the tone of American officials have (sic) become harsher and more insulting."[16] With help from Iran and Turkey unlikely, arming and supporting the Kurdish Peshmerga and the Iraqi army and hoping for the best and preparing for the worst is the backup.

Option Four: Orchestrate humanitarian aid to the trapped Iraqis, create a safe corridor to evacuate them and continue to harass ISIS fighters from the air. This option is not a slam-dunk. Creating the safe corridor is not easy and will require boots on the ground as well as air support. Who will supply the boots on the ground is unclear. An ongoing air campaign against ISIS also will increase the likelihood that expat fighters from western countries will become determined to strike back in their home countries.

Most importantly, the U.S. needs to decide on the strategic goal. Is the goal to stabilize Iraq as a cohesive unit, accept that Iraq will break up and shepherd this transition or conduct a strictly humanitarian intervention and let the Iraqis figure it out for themselves. Once we understand the goal we can assess the resources necessary to accomplish it and decide whether or not we are willing to deploy them. My sense is that we should try to maintain Iraq as a state, support regional and local forces in this effort and be prepared for the worst. What do you think?

Is the Civil War in Syria Reaching a Tipping Point?
(Blog from 5/30/2015)

For the last four years the bloody Syrian Civil War has evolved into a multi-party stalemate with small pieces of territory shifting back and forth between the competing forces and with the ongoing killing of fighters and civilians. Recent events may portend a change in this dynamic. On May 21st Islamic State (IS) forces pushed Syrian government forces out of the ancient city of Palmyra and took control of the strategically located city. While the mainstream media focused attention on the ancient ruins in the UNESCO World Heritage site and the fate of the endangered Arabian Ibis, the potential implications of this event for the medium and long-term dynamics of the war have largely gone unexamined.

Palmyra, located in the geographic center of Syria, astride a major highway linking Iraq in the east with the more populated portions of Syria in the west, is geographically situated as a major hub for military deployment. The political and military dynamics that led to the fall of Palmyra also shed light on the shifting power balance in Syria. The shifting balance not only has military implications, but also, and perhaps more importantly, significant psychological implications for the minority populations in Syria.

Since the beginning of the war, the strategy (if you can call it that) of the U.S. and its western and regional allies has been to harass IS forces from the air and to arm and train so-called moderate opposition forces in Syria opposed to the Assad-led government. This internally contradictory policy has led to a bizarre scenario in which the U.S. fights Assad on one hand and supports him in his battle with IS on the other. The results of this policy have had a negative impact on the Syrian government's ability to confront IS forces.

The U.S. does not use air strikes to support Assad forces in their battle with IS. It does, however, support the "moderate" rebel forces and the Kurdish militias against IS. This has led IS to conclude that, although it doesn't have a primary objective of overthrowing Assad, it is safer to concentrate its efforts against the Syrian government forces. The policy also has encouraged the Army of Conquest, an alliance among various Islamist groups, including the al-Qaeda-linked al-Nusra Front and the Muslim Brotherhood-affiliated Faylaq al-Sham and other smaller groups backed by Qatar, Saudi Arabia and Turkey. Combining this strengthening of opposition forces with the difficulty that Assad is experiencing in replacing the manpower lost, puts the Syrian government in an increasingly difficult position. This played out in Palmyra when government forces were shifted from Palmyra to Idlib to confront a growing rebel threat. This depleted the forces in Palmyra and IS took advantage of the situation to take over the city. Now in control of this central location IS is well positioned to take advantage of similar situations in the future.

The changing dynamic also puts Assad allies, Iran and Hezbollah, in a difficult position. Unless they are willing and able to go all out to defend the Assad regime, they may need to recognize reality, commit to defending Lebanon and accept the breakup of Iraq into Kurdistan, IS and Shiastan in southern Iraq.

If the Assad regime does collapse, it likely will happen quickly as minority Alawites, Druze and Christians lose confidence that Assad will survive and choose to flee rather than wait for the inevitable ethnic and religious cleansing and genocide. An influx of massive numbers of refugees into Jordan, Lebanon and Iraq will surely destabilize these already weak countries. The alliances of convenience among disparate groups in Syria will, inevitably, break down leading to the total collapse of the state and to the rise of fiefdoms ruled by gangsters, warlords and religious fanatics. When a policy that makes no sense actually succeeds, the outcome is generally not pretty.

The Yemen Civil War

The best way to understand Yemen is to acknowledge that it is not a country, but rather a collection of tribes. Periodically, outside powers such as the Ottomans and the British have tried unsuccessfully to subdue the tribes and establish control enough to achieve their political and economic goals. Since the 1960s, Yemen has been in a state of almost continual civil war. Although the fighting has ebbed and flowed over the years, periods of stability have been rare.

The current iteration of Yemeni Civil War has its roots in the Arab Spring with the 2011 Yemen Intifada (uprising) that demanded the resignation of longtime President Ali Abdullah Saleh. In the course of the intifada, many military officers and government officials defected to the opposition and the government lost control of much of the country. Concerned about instability in a neighboring country, the Gulf Cooperation Council brokered a deal under which Saleh would turn power over to his Vice President Abd Rabbuh Mansur Hadi in return for immunity. The deal was accepted by Saleh, but rejected by many in the opposition, most importantly the Houthi tribe based in northern Yemen.

The Houthis, who are Zaidi or Fiver Shia Muslims based in the mountains of northern Yemen, along the border with Saudi Arabia, have long had a strained relationship with the Sunni-dominated government in Sana'a. They have felt that the oil wealth, such as it is, has disproportionately benefited the Sunni areas of Yemen. In 2014, after several weeks of protest against the Hadi government, Houthi forces in an unlikely alliance with forces loyal to former President Saleh, directly engaged and defeated forces loyal to Hadi. The Houthis quickly captured Sana'a and established a Revolutionary Council that included other tribes opposed to the Hadi government. Throughout 2014 and early 2015 forces allied with the Houthis advanced southward capturing much of western Yemen including the strategic port of Aden.

The U.S. has long had a presence in Yemen conducting counter terrorism operations (primarily drone strikes), against al-Qaeda in the Arabian Peninsula (AQAP). The U.S., having lost its ally President Saleh as a result of the uprisings of the Arab Spring, concerned that ungoverned areas of southern Yemen caused by the overthrow of the Saleh government would provide a refuge for AQAP and ISIS, worried about increased Iranian influence with the Shia Houthis in power, began to search for "good guys" to support in order to stabilize the situation. The problem was "there are no good guys." Enter the Saudis.

Saudi Arabia's relationship with the Houthis has been troubled for many years. The Saudis have been concerned about Houthi and Iranian influence with their own oppressed and restive Shia population in the oil rich eastern provinces. Houthis have resisted, sometimes violently, Saudi attempts to introduce their intolerant, conservative Wahhabi version of Sunni Islam into their more relaxed Shia culture. In March

2015, Saudi Arabia, allied with other GCC countries, intervened in the civil war. The intervention has largely consisted of air strikes and blockades that have created a significant humanitarian crisis in already impoverished Yemen. In support of the intervention, the U.S. has provided intelligence, logistical and mid-air refueling assistance. After some initial success the operation has bogged down into a stalemate with no signs of resolution. Meanwhile AQAP and ISIS have expanded their areas of influence.

How We Got Here:

Six Things You Need to Know About the War in Yemen
(Blog from 5/1/2015)

As the conflict in Yemen has transitioned from an insurgency against the central government in Sana'a by the northern tribes led by Abdul-Malik al-Houthi, into a civil war, a number of outside players have joined the fight. This has made the situation much more complicated. Americans have a habit of seeing all conflict and instability in binomial terms. There is a presumption (as noted above) that the sides in any conflict can be divided into "good guys" and "bad guys" and that the U.S. should intervene on behalf of the good side. Usually, though, the situation is much more complicated and nuanced and many times there are no "good guys." This is particularly true in Yemen. Consider these:

1. The war is not a sectarian conflict. The Houthis have, for years, harbored legitimate grievances involving the distribution of resources and power within Yemen. Their grievances have been shared by other northern tribes. This accounts for the broad-based support for the insurgency and for its rapid success. The Houthis have a broad base of popular support throughout Yemen and will be very difficult to defeat, even with outside intervention. Houthi ability to protect communities against the advance of al-Qaeda, achieve a level of political participation and root out corruption has only enhanced their popularity.

2. The Houthis are not a client of Iran. The Houthi relationship with Iran has been overstated by Saudi Arabia, which has tried to frame the conflict as a Sunni-Shia conflict, and as an existential threat

to Sunni monarchies. Houthis are Zaidis (Fiver) Shias, whereas Iranians are Twelver Shias. To frame the difference in Christian terms, Twelvers are Church of England and Fivers are Pentecostal. They are both Protestant, but you wouldn't know it by looking at their beliefs and practices. As with Hezbollah in Lebanon, Houthis are a Yemeni movement supported financially, politically and sometimes militarily, by Iran. Iran supports the Houthi movement because an independent, inclusive government in Yemen would remove another Arab state that might ally with its adversaries. This support, however, does not necessarily translate into control over Houthi activities.

3. This is not a binomial conflict. The Houthis have a very bad relationship with al-Qaeda in the Arabian Peninsula (AQAP) and the Islamic State. Saudi Arabia, Jorden, UAE and, to some extent, the U.S., have intervened on behalf of the internationally recognized government of Abd Hadi, AQAP and the Islamic State. The southern tribes quietly have been waiting on the sidelines, ready to take advantage of any chance to assert their independence. The motivations of these outside forces are not ones that the U.S. should be associating itself with. There are no "good guys."

4. The Houthis don't want to govern Yemen; they just don't want anyone else to govern it either. They are interested in a high degree of autonomy and local issues prevail over national issues.

5. The war is remaking the regional geopolitical system. As Saudi Arabia has attempted to assemble a coalition to confront the Houthi movement and its allies, one key player is missing. Pakistan, a long-time military ally of Saudi Arabia, has elected to remain neutral. As relations between Iran and the U.S. appear to be improving, much to the dismay of Jerusalem and Riyadh, Pakistan, with a long border with Iran, may be reconsidering its geopolitical alignment. An emboldened Iran, with the ability to peel away Sunni countries from the Saudi Arabia-led alliance system, does not bode well for Riyadh's geopolitical goals.

6. Saudi Arabia's intervention in Yemen is very risky. The bombing campaign alone is unlikely to achieve the Saudi-stated objective of creating a "stable and safe" Yemen. Eventually, a major ground incursion will be required. The Houthis, intimately familiar with the mountainous terrain, able to use the terrain effectively to confront an invading

conventional army and to provide refuge against air attacks, will be very difficult to defeat. The inevitable collateral civilian casualties resulting from the air campaign will increase the local popularity of the Houthi, who can portray themselves as defending Yemen against an invading foreign army. Yemenis will remember the Egyptian air campaign during the Saudi-Egyptian proxy war in Yemen during the 1960s. Both Egypt and Saudi Arabia are playing with fire. Yemen, like Afghanistan, has shown itself to be the graveyard of empires.

The situation in Yemen is a complicated conflict largely driven by long-standing local grievances and animosities. Saudi Arabia has intervened in order to prevent an independent government that they are unable to control from taking power right next door. Why the U.S. would want to get involved at all, since there is no national interest at stake, is unclear. We would be better off telling the Saudis that if they get themselves in trouble, they are on their own.

CHAPTER 5

The Clash Between Power and Independence

America's efforts to project power and to influence political events and decisions have clashed with the desire of Middle Eastern countries to retain their traditional culture and political independence. When Americans use the phrase "that's history," the underlying meaning is that it is irrelevant. But in many parts of the world, including the Middle East, history is everything. The historical legacy of colonialism in the region has made the Middle Eastern countries very sensitive to issues that impinge on their sovereign right to make their own policy choices.

The region of the world that we now call the Near East or the Middle East has been dominated, to a greater or lesser degree, by outside forces from the time the armies of Islam swept out of the Arabian Peninsula in 632 CE. The Muslims rapidly conquered most of the Middle East and North Africa and established the Umayyad Dynasty in 661CE. The region was ruled by a series of Islamic Caliphates until the late 18th Century. European domination came after Napoleon's expedition to Egypt in 1798. Shortly after that expedition the British and the Ottomans, at various times working together, forced Napoleon to withdraw from Egypt and restored Ottoman rule. Over the next 100 years the British and the Ottomans vied for power in Egypt and the Levant.

The French retained control of most of the rest of North Africa. Following WWI, under the 1916 Sykes-Picot Agreement, the British and the French divided up the remainder of the Ottoman Empire into colonial mandates approved by the League of Nations. As part of the process of promoting the Arab revolt against the Ottomans, the British and French deceived the Arab leaders about their intention to establish an independent Arab state. To this day these actions have not been forgiven—or forgotten. The colonial borders established by Sykes-Picot were drawn with little regard for tribal and ethnic considerations and were designed to divide and rule. These divisions, for the most part, survived as national borders when many of the colonies gained independence during the period 1945-1960.

As the areas of the region became independent as European-style nation states, nationalism began to succeed religion, ethnicity and tribalism as the uniting factor. With their colonial history, these new nation states have made political independence a priority.

This dynamic has manifested itself in the modern politics of the region. The total U.S. withdrawal from Iraq was the result of a disagreement over whether or not U.S. troops should be immune from the sovereign jurisdiction of Iraqi courts. Egypt's leaders often have accused foreigners of working covertly to destabilize Egypt during its transition to democracy. When U.S. NGOs (non-governmental organizations) went to Egypt to assist in democracy building following the 2011 revolution, they were greeted with distrust and some were arrested. Middle Eastern leaders are wary of the intentions of the western imperial powers and persuasion has not been an effective tool to elicit support for U.S. interests.

Arab populations viewed the establishment of the state of Israel by a UN dominated by the western colonial powers as another colonial project and an effort to bring European settlers onto Arab lands. Despite a completely different history from its Arab neighbors, Israel, America's staunchest ally, has also been reluctant to accommodate U.S. interests. Moshe Dayan, Israel's Minister of Defense from 1967-1974 and Minister of Foreign Affairs from 1977-1979, once said, "Our American friends offer us money, arms, and advice. We take the money, we take the arms, and we decline the advice." As recently as 2012, Israeli Prime Minister Netanyahu said, "When it comes to Israel's security, Israel has the sovereign right to make its own decisions."

According to former Secretary of State Hillary Clinton, U.S. ally,

Saudi Arabia, is the largest source of funds for the Sunni militant groups Al Qaeda and the Taliban. She said, "Donors in Saudi Arabia constitute the most significant source of funding to Sunni terrorist groups worldwide." Despite U.S. criticism and exhortation, Saudi Arabia and other Gulf State allies have been one of the main sources of funding for ISIS. Although these activities increase security threats to the U.S., the U.S. continues to sell high-tech weaponry to Saudi Arabia. *The New York Times* reported, "The Defense Department is expected to finalize a $10 billion arms deal with Israel, Saudi Arabia and the United Arab Emirates next week (April 2013) that will provide missiles, warplanes and troop transports to help them counter any future threat from Iran."

Iran, during the long arduous negotiations over its nuclear program, the EU3+3 insisted on recognition of its right, as a signatory of the Nuclear Non-proliferation Treaty (NPT), to a peaceful nuclear program including a mastery of the complete fuel cycle. In order to achieve the agreement that insured that the program was peaceful, the U.S. and its negotiating partners, after years of insisting that the entire nuclear program be dismantled, were forced to acknowledge that Iran could retain its program.

The U.S. has continued its support of Israel and Saudi Arabia despite their reluctance to support American interests and policy preferences. Professor Margaret Macmillan of Oxford University points out in a Brookings Institution essay, "...patron nations are reluctant to abandon their clients, no matter how far they have run amok and no matter what dangers they themselves are being led into, because to do so incurs the risk of making the greater power appear weak and indecisive. Great powers often face the dilemma that their very support for smaller ones encourages their clients to be reckless. And their clients often slip the leading strings of their patrons...The region (Middle East) has seized control of its own politics. It must now take responsibility for its economics. No government in the region is prepared now to entrust its future to foreigners, still less to a single foreign power."

The people of the region are beginning to realize that with sovereignty and with political independence come responsibility. After a decade plus of nation-building efforts in Iraq and Afghanistan, the U.S. has been forced to realize that only the Iraqis and Afghans can build their own nations. We can help them make a better nation, but only they can build their nation. The U.S. spent $50 billion on "nation building" in Iraq and it didn't work. Before you can build a nation, you have to have a nation and only the citizens of that nation can decide what kind of a country they want to have.

Even Israel, whose character has been shaped by European nationalism, is struggling with the decision of what kind of a state it wants to be. Israel's leaders have attempted to get Palestine and other Arab states to recognize Israel as a "Jewish state." The reality is that only Israel can decide if it is a Jewish state and the status of non-Jews in a Jewish state.

How We Got Here:

Ignoring Advice (Blog from 12/14/2006)

In 2003, a year after the U.S. invasion of Iraq, I made a trip to Jordan to help build a house with Habitat for Humanity International. I was touring the sights of Jordan with a guide who had attended college in Baghdad during the regime of Saddam Hussein. Sami and I were discussing the Iraq war and its impact. This was a time when almost everybody, including myself, felt that we were making progress toward a democratic Iraqi state that would be a positive force for a more peaceful Middle East. Sami's reaction was that Saddam Hussein was a really bad guy and the Middle East was better off without him, but he also said he would have preferred the Iraqis to have handled Hussein themselves. He said, "You guys have no idea what you are getting into. There are 1,300 different ethnic, sectarian, tribal and political groups in Iraq. Without a really strong leader there isn't a country there." How prescient he was.

The concept of a "nation state" is very much a western concept. In the Middle East people relate much more to the Umma (the Muslim community) and to their tribe. When Gertrude Bell drew the lines in the Middle East after WWI, she not only brought the western idea of a nation state and the political and imperialist expectations of the victors to the process, but also a very British penchant for straight lines. Although she understood the area better than almost anybody else, she ended up with Arabs, Kurds, Persians, Sunni, Shia, Christians, Druze, etc. scattered among the countries of the region. It makes the Balkans look like a unified society. The Iraq Study Group seemed to implicitly recognize this reality by inserting this caveat after they opposed devolution of Iraq into three regions: "...if events were to move irreversibly in this direction (i.e. devolution), the United States should manage the situation to ameliorate humanitarian consequences, contain the spread of violence and minimize regional instability."

In the recent mid-term election, the American people expressed strongly that they weren't satisfied with our policy in Iraq. Since satisfaction is the difference between expectations and reality, George Bush seems to have decided that it is better to improve satisfaction by lowering expectations than by changing the reality. We have come from defining success as a "free and democratic Iraq that is an ally in the 'war on terror' and a model for the 'new Middle East'" to an Iraq that "can govern itself, sustain itself and defend itself." The Iraq Study Group has made a number of suggestions about how to improve the reality on the ground, but George Bush appears to be about to ignore most of them. He would not be the first recent President to ignore the recommendations of the bi-partisan study group designed to give him political cover for difficult decisions. In 1998, President Clinton appointed a bi-partisan commission headed by moderate Louisiana Senator John Breaux to recommend changes necessary to prevent the bankruptcy of the Medicare program. When the commission issued its report, Clinton ignored the whole thing. I'll grant that he was a little preoccupied with Monica at the time, but he might have done something with it. Even though George Bush doesn't have an intern problem, he is probably going to cherry pick a few recommendations about technical and political assistance, call it good and end up "staying the course." Since he doesn't have to check this out with the American people at the ballot box, he is likely to show his usual stubbornness. His Republican supporters who do have to run again may start heading for the exits. Meanwhile, while the politicians dither, America's sons and daughters are still dying to try to create a reality that may not exist.

Illogical Thinking (Blog from 9/18/2007)

As part of their campaign to justify invading Iraq, the U.S. government maintained that Saddam Hussein's government was aiding al-Qaeda and would provide them with "weapons of mass destruction" (WMD) from their non-existent stockpiles. I believed the assertion that Iraq had WMD; after all it was a "slam dunk." (Is it ever?) However, the al-Qaeda claim never made sense to me. al-Qaeda's ultimate goal is to establish a Sunni Muslim caliphate in the Middle East and more ambitiously in the world. Saddam Hussein was a secular Ba'athist Socialist. The last thing he would want to see was an Islamic government in the Middle East. Now, in making the case for war in Iran, the U.S. is accusing Iran of supporting the Taliban in Afghanistan and aiding insurgent groups in Iraq. The Taliban claim also makes no sense to me as it is a long-standing supporter of Al-Qaeda and also wants to see a Sunni Islamic caliphate. Iran is a Shia country and considers the Taliban a dangerous adversary. Based on this view, Iran aided U.S. efforts to overthrow the Taliban in Afghanistan. Iran also has poor relations with Pakistan, a supporter of the Taliban, and an ally of the U.S. (Huh??) As an Iranian government minister said after Pakistan exploded its first nuclear weapon, "That was a genie that would have been best left in the bottle." Why would Iran want to support the Taliban efforts to reestablish an enemy state right on its borders? Again, this makes little sense. In terms of Iranian activity in Iraq, the Shia groups that Iran has the most influence with are the Islamic Supreme Council of Iraq and al-Dawa. Both of these groups are part of the U.S.-supported government of Prime Minister Nouri al-Maliki. Muqtada al-Sadr's Mahdi Army has more of an Iraqi nationalist agenda and is probably not a strong client of Iran. Although weapons may flow across the long and porous border between Iran and Iraq and the Iranian government has many factions with different agendas, it is hard to imagine that the Iranian government would support insurgents fighting against a government made up of the people with whom it has the best relations.

Perhaps one of the lessons learned from the Iraq war debacle is that if it doesn't make sense, perhaps it isn't true no matter how many times the U.S. government says it.

The Afghan Dilemma (Blog from 12/8/2009)

In December 2009, President Obama outlined his so-called "surge and exit" strategy for turning around the deteriorating situation in the then 8-year war in Afghanistan. The surge side of the equation is being promptly implemented by the U.S. and its European allies. The exit side is a little more problematic. Faced with criticism from Republican hawks, Secretary of Defense Gates and Secretary of State Clinton attempted to frame the July 2011 "exit" date as a decision point rather than a hard date for withdrawal. The major accomplishment of the "new" is to kick the can down the road.

Given the fact that the Army/Marine Corp counter insurgency manual, authored by current CentCom commander General David Petraeus, calls for troop levels somewhere north of 600,000 and a 7-10-year time frame, one might be forgiven for being skeptical of an 18-month turnaround with 150,000 troops.

The strategy outlined by the administration is reminiscent of the Soviet Union strategy during its ill-fated Afghanistan escapade in the 1980s; control and stabilize the population centers and the highways connecting them and rely on a puppet government in Kabul to take over. While there are similarities to the failed Soviet campaign, there are also differences. The U.S. is not faced with an insurgent force armed and equipped by a major power providing them with Stinger missiles and thus is able to control the air. The U.S. is also attempting to rebuild the country and not destroy it. On the other side, the Soviets were relying on a much more competent government in Kabul.

On balance, the U.S. will probably succeed in stabilizing some population centers and forcing the insurgents into Pakistan and the Afghan countryside where they can be harassed from the air. The major risk to this plan is that in 18 months we will see some progress and the military will come back to Obama and say, "See, we are making progress. Just give us another 50,000 troops and another two years and we can 'win.'" It will be hard for Obama to say no!

I am old enough to remember Vietnam where steady escalation of troops, casualties, and financial commitment finally led to the conclusion that the war was un-winnable. Obama had only bad choices, but he picked the worst of the bunch.

Afghan Politics (Blog from 6/24/2011)

When I was visiting the Persian Gulf region in 2011, I had a conversation with a senior Middle East analyst at the State Department. I asked him why it is that, when the professionals in the State Department clearly understand the realities on the ground, United States policy in the region is so disconnected from reality. He replied that the job of the professionals was to provide analysis of the situation and policy recommendations, however, the policy makers are political appointees and therefore, policy decisions are generally based on domestic political considerations rather than reality on the ground. We saw this dynamic play out in June 2011 with the announcement of U.S. policy in Afghanistan.

President Obama in his policy speech described the success of American counter-terrorism efforts and said that he planned to continue them. He said, "al-Qaeda is under more pressure than at any time since 9/11," "al-Qaeda is under enormous strain," and "We have put al-Qaeda on a path to defeat and we will not relent..." Prior to the speech a senior administration official said that the government had not seen a "terrorist threat" from Afghanistan in seven or eight years. He also said that only 50 to 75 al Qaeda members remain in Afghanistan.

Obama also disavowed a counter-insurgency and nation-building strategy saying, "We will not try to make Afghanistan a perfect place. We will not police its streets or patrol its mountains...That is the responsibility of the Afghan government..."

Given his counter-terrorism strategy, the extended withdrawal timeframe (extending at least through 2014) makes little sense tactically. A counter-terrorism approach could be implemented with drones and Special Forces, allowing an immediate large scale withdrawal. Politically, however, it makes a lot of sense. A significant withdrawal will occur right before the 2012 elections and the remaining withdrawals are extended over years. By walking the middle ground, as is his penchant, Obama inoculates himself against attacks by the doves, who want a quick withdrawal, and the hawks who want a continuing major military presence.

It remains to be seen how the Taliban will react. They operate on a long-term horizon. I once heard author Greg Mortenson, author of *Three Cups of Tea*, describe a Taliban plan to recruit the best and brightest young children from Afghan villages, indoctrinate them in Pakistani madrassas, send them back to the villages to marry four wives and have as many children as they can. That is a really long-range plan! The Taliban use a saying, "You have the watch. We have the time."

Afghanistan after America (Blog from 10/18/2012)

With all the loud and largely fact free debate that went on during the 2012 presidential campaign, very little was said about America's longest war in Afghanistan. Neither candidate wanted to talk about it since a reluctant Obama was never really sold on the surge strategy and any position taken by Romney would tie his hands should he be elected. After his victory, Obama was faced with some very difficult decisions. With the 2014 deadline for withdrawal of American combat forces and a massive logistical task required to implement an orderly withdrawal, decisions will need to be made quickly. Since the press is preoccupied with campaign non-events, it might be useful to look at where we are and what the future might bring.

I attended a recent conference on the subject where Ryan Crocker, recently retired ambassador to Afghanistan, Iraq and four other Middle East countries, expressed his view that the surge had been relatively successful. Since Ambassador Crocker is no Pollyanna, (he was sarcastically dubbed "sunshine" by President Bush for ongoing pessimistic reports on the situation in Iraq) his assessment should be taken seriously.

While poorly conceived, planned and implemented, the surge still has accomplished some of its objectives. The surge forces have gained control of major population centers and the roads connecting them. While it might have been more useful to train fewer forces better, 350,000 Afghan security forces have been partially trained and they may be capable of sustaining some control of the population centers once U.S. forces have departed. Some economic development projects have been completed. However, the vast majority of Afghan GDP (Gross Domestic Product) is still directly tied to western aid and the presence of thousands of foreign troops and civilian workers. All this has been achieved in the face of rampant corruption, incompetence and bureaucratic infighting between the Department of State and the Pentagon, within the armed services and among allies. No small accomplishment. It is possible that we might just muddle through.

Nonetheless, everything must go exactly right over the next few years for this not to be a complete disaster. Some of the factors we have some control over and some we do not. It should be noted that Murphy probably developed his law after observing Afghanistan. Some of the factors to watch for are:

- Are the Afghan security forces as good as Crocker thinks they are?

- The Afghan political situation is fragile. Will Hamid Karzai step down at the end of his term? Who will succeed him?

- What will Iran do? In the current circumstance, Iran is incentivized to maintain managed chaos.

- What will Pakistan do? Pakistan will not allow an Indian client state on its western border. The good news on this front is that the Pakistani public no longer sees India as the major threat. America has assumed this position.

America East of Suez (Blog from 10/29/2013)

Last week President Obama's National Security Adviser, Susan Rice, unveiled, what the media is calling "a more modest strategy for the Mideast."[17] Ms. Rice said that the administration would focus its efforts on negotiating a nuclear deal with Iran, brokering a peace agreement between Israel and the Palestinians and mitigating the strife in Syria. The strategy also acknowledged that there are limits to what the U.S. can accomplish in nurturing democracy in the region. While I might argue with some of the specifics, the new strategy appears to be an effort to rectify some of the problems that have plagued U.S. policy in the Middle East for decades.

As U.S. involvement in the Middle East has deepened since the end of WWII, U.S. efforts to project power in the region have clashed with the desire of Middle Easterners for self-determination and political independence. The U.S. also has failed to identify its vital national interests and to focus its policies and power on addressing those interests. This lack of focus has led to policies and objectives that are not only conflicting, but in many cases mutually exclusive. These policy disconnects have led to a failure to accomplish foreign policy objectives. Those it has accomplished have been more in spite of rather than because of the policies.

My definition of a "vital national interest" is one that deals with an existential threat to the U.S. and one for which the U.S. is willing to spill its blood and to spend its treasure in order to accomplish its objectives. By this definition, the U.S. has no vital national interest in events in the Middle East. Since WWII access to the energy resources of the Middle East at a reasonable price has been a vital national interest. With the advent of "fracking" and shale, the U.S. is on the verge of becoming a net energy exporter and this has fundamentally changed energy geopolitics. U.S. interests are now more associated with non-proliferation of WMD and controlling and defeating the Sunni jihadist threat. While U.S. blind support for Israel will remain a thorn in the side of the U.S. as it attempts to deal with Middle Easterners, the larger Israeli/Palestinian conflict, with the death of the two-state solution, has morphed into an internal Israeli problem. The Israelis themselves will have to decide what kind of a country they want to be.

The Obama administration seems to have realized that, in order to deal successfully with the jihadist and WMD issues, it will need to deal with Iran. Iranian cooperation is crucial for the attainment of U.S. policy objectives. Success in dealing with Iran will require taking into account Iran's requirement for sovereignty over its energy policy and autonomy in designing and implementing its foreign policy. Saudi Arabia has become marginalized on the energy issue and on the jihadist issue. It is part of the problem and not part of the solution. Saudi realization that the U.S. may be looking after its own national interest rather than following the lead of the most undemocratic regimes in the region has led to what only can be described as a "temper tantrum."

Turning down a seat on the UN Security Council[18] to send a message to the U.S. may be the ultimate tantrum.

The U.S. may be experiencing its own "East of Suez" moment as it accepts that it has diminished influence in the global arena.[19] This transition will be difficult for Americans to accept, particularly the empire building neo-cons, but at the end of the day both America and the Middle East may be better for it.

Nuclear Negotiations: An Iranian Perspective
(Blog from 11/28/2014)

This week the year-long negotiations between Iran and the major powers regarding the Iranian nuclear program ended in failure. The most that the negotiators could accomplish was to agree to continue talking for another seven months. When the negotiation process was extended in July 2014, many observers, myself included, were optimistic that an agreement was possible. I wrote at the time, "Once the July 20 'deadline' passes, the negotiators will be faced with the brutal reality that this is the last, best chance to contain Iran's nuclear program without military action and a likely regional war." Unfortunately, it now appears that there is no overlap in the positions of the two sides. The most that the Iranians are willing to give with regard to restraints on their nuclear program is less that the U.S. is willing to accept and the most that the U.S. is willing to give with regard to sanctions relief is less than the Iranians are willing to accept. We now face the reality of a long period of difficult negotiations if we are to achieve a peaceful solution. While most western media coverage has been focused on U.S. demands and politics, the Iranian perspective is at least as important. In order to understand the Iranian position we need to examine culture, internal politics, economics and regional and global geopolitics.

1. Culture: Iran, having a long, proud Persian history, united by a common Shiite religious tradition, even though being culturally and ethnically diverse, is able to maintain a powerful sense of nationalism. Looking back on their ancient Persian history, Iranians strongly support

their "rightful" position as a regional power. Ninety percent of Iranians are members of the Shiite branch of Islam and, as such, see themselves as followers of Imam Hussein, the grandson of the Prophet Muhammad and the third Shia Imam, who was killed and beheaded by the Umayyad caliph in 680 CE in Karbala in present day Iraq. This event, commemorated by Shia Muslims each year in a Day of Mourning (Ashura), instills in Shiites a strong sense of sacrifice, even to the point of martyrdom, in defense of a just cause. These cultural factors make it unlikely that Iranians will be bullied into giving up their rights under the NPT (Treaty on the Non-Proliferation of Nuclear Weapons) by the threat of harsh sanctions.

2. Politics: Domestic politics also greatly affects how Iranian leaders deal with the U.S. and the nuclear issue. In broad terms, the Iranian political landscape, as in the U.S., is divided into two camps: the traditionalists (principlists), who oppose any compromise or engagement with the West and the modernists (reformists) who favor engagement and flexibility in dealing with the West. These two camps compete for influence with the Supreme Leader who is the ultimate decision maker in national security affairs. President Hassan Rouhani, an experienced political player in the Iranian system, while leaning toward the reformist camp, tries to have one foot down in each camp. The extension of the talks into 2015 has brought them right into the middle of the political posturing going into Iran's parliamentary elections. The failure of the negotiations, a major part of Rouhani's engagement platform, will give the principlists backing for their position that "negotiations with the U.S. are a waste of time, as the U.S. policies will never change." As an Iranian source told me, "It is a reasonable estimate that the next parliament might have a different setting." A more hostile Parliament will make it very difficult for Rouhani to keep his U.S.-educated, fluent-English speaking Foreign Minister, Javad

Zarif, in power. Widely ignored in the Western media, but perhaps more important than the Parliamentary election, is the 2016 election of the Assembly of Experts. Among other responsibilities, the Assembly of Experts is tasked with choosing the Supreme leader. With Supreme Leader Ali Khamenei being 78 years old and seemingly in poor health, this Assembly of Experts is almost certain to select the next Supreme Leader. The worldview of this person will affect U.S./Iran relations for years to come.

3.   Economics: Following the collapse of the nuclear talks, Republicans in the U.S. Congress have wasted no time in threatening additional economic sanctions on Iran. Ignoring the issues of the perception in Iran that sanctions are intended to destabilize the Iranian political system and the unwillingness of Iran to continue negotiations under threat, the economic impact of sanctions on ordinary Iranians is diverse. There are winners and losers. The winners from continued sanctions are those who profit from the major enterprises involved in skirting sanction, including, but not limited to, the Iranian Revolutionary Guard, as well as private businesses protected from global competition by the sanction restrictions. Perhaps surprisingly, other winners are the growing number of tech entrepreneurs who are able to clone western tech products and build their businesses without fear of competition from large western companies. Among the losers are those who depend on imported products either for sale or as components, those needing western medical products and those who wish to partner and to expand globally. The point is that there is a, not insignificant, constituency supporting isolation from the west and building, what the Supreme Leader calls a "resistance economy."

4.   Geopolitics: As Iran's leaders look out at the world around them, they can't help but conclude that the arc of history is bending in their direction. Regionally, as

Shia populations become more assertive, Iran's relations with Iraq, Syria, Lebanon and Yemen have rarely been stronger. Iran's rivals, such as Saudi Arabia, Israel, Bahrain and Egypt, faced with increasing internal dissent and unrest, are being forced to turn inward and to deal with their own problems. Globally Russia and China, increasingly realizing that the U.S. has the ability to deploy, what I call, the financial neutron bomb, using the dollar denominated global financial system to destroy a country's economy, have begun to get serious about establishing an alternative system. Such an alternative system cannot but help Iran deal with U.S. sanctions. Seeing the racially and economically divided U.S. politically gridlocked and the economically stagnant European Union more divided than united, Iran must conclude, "time is on our side."

Barring a major turnabout by either side, it seems unlikely that another seven months of talking will change the outcome. For Iranians no deal may be better than a bad deal. We may have missed, and maybe lost, "the last, best chance to contain Iran's nuclear program without military action and a likely regional war."

Will the Iran Nuclear Deal Change the Geopolitics of the Middle East? (Blog from 9/8/2015)

As the September 17, 2015 deadline for Congress to act on the Iran Nuclear Agreement (JCPOA) approaches, the media has been flooded with editorials, op-ed pieces and blogs making the case for or against the agreement. Those in favor of the agreement have made the case that, while an imperfect agreement, the deal was the best that could be achieved and, through intrusive inspections, will ensure that Iran's nuclear program will remain peaceful and will not achieve a nuclear weapon. Those opposed have made arguments such as: "It's Iran, we can't deal with them, we just like sanctions, Iran shouldn't have any nuclear capability, Iran is Israel's enemy," and the agreement only lasts 15 years. Both sides of the debate seem to acknowledge that this agreement will drastically change the geopolitics of the Middle East. But, is this really true?

The underlying assumption of those critical of a change in the geopolitical alignment is that the current alignment has been successful in maintaining peace and stability and promoting economic growth, a dubious proposition at best. Those in favor of a geopolitical realignment see a new world in which Iran becomes an important player in bringing stability and order out of the current chaos. While this new world would certainly be an improvement over the current situation, there are a number of reasons to be skeptical of the chances for realignment.

First, and probably most important, is that one of the founding principles of the Islamic Republic of Iran was resistance to U.S. domination of the region. The U.S. and Iran are fundamentally at odds over the geopolitics of the Middle East. While the administration of President Hassan Rouhani is more open to engagement with the west, any thought that Iran will give up its independent foreign policy and follow the American lead is unrealistic. Iran and the U.S. may cooperate on issues where their interests align (Afghanistan, ISIS, drug trafficking, etc.) but Iran will continue to lead the so-called "axis of resistance" and that will not sit well with U.S. policy makers.

Second, the much-discussed idea that Israel will react to the nuclear deal by allying itself with Saudi Arabia and Hamas in opposition to Iran is also unrealistic. Despite all the rumors of high level meetings, it is hard to see how Saudi Arabia, whose radically conservative Wahhabi version of Islam provides the ideological underpinning for the Islamic State (ISIS), can ever align itself with Israel. With respect to Hamas, the ceasefire agreement between Israel and the Hamas government in Gaza is getting long in the tooth. Israel has not implemented much of what it agreed to and thus the same conditions of poverty, deprivation and lack of hope that led to the last two wars still exist in Gaza. The next war may not be far away.

Third, despite the best efforts of Russia, Iran and the U.S., the situation in Syria will remain a festering sore and a source of instability and chaos. It is hard to see a solution. With major regional players such as Turkey, Saudi Arabia and Kuwait seeing the region through a sectarian lens, committed to the overthrow of the government of

Syrian President Assad and, at best, ambivalent about ISIS, a coalition of western and regional powers to stabilize Syria is very unlikely. As long as ISIS remains in place, a solution to Iraq's collapse as a contiguous and sovereign state is impossible and the Kurdish problem will remain unresolved.

Fourth, the window of opportunity to realign the Middle East will soon close. Whatever the outcome of the upcoming U.S. elections and given the influence of the Israel lobby on U.S. Middle East policy, the next administration is likely to be less open to growing Iranian influence in the region. Israel will certainly not elect a more accommodating government. Whatever *rapprochement* is achieved by the Obama administration in its last year in office, will be short lived. Iran, seeing its hopes of greater integration with the West dashed and strengthened by the removal of sanctions will be forced to look east to Russia and China for allies.

In 2006, Secretary of State Condoleezza Rice, following the U.S. invasion and destruction of Iraq and Israel's destruction of Gaza, famously declared the destruction of Lebanon by Israel as the "birth pangs of the new Middle East" and confirmed the U.S. policy of "creative chaos," in which the old order is destroyed and in its place a new order arises which will serve the goals of U.S. policy. The U.S., having created the "new Middle East," will have to live with the consequences for some time.

CHAPTER 6
Unintended Consequences

When I attended a conference with Ryan Crocker, former U.S. Ambassador to Iraq and Afghanistan under the George W. Bush and Obama administrations, he said that he had three rules when considering whether or not to intervene in another country's affairs. They are:

1. Be very careful before you get in.

2. Be aware of unintended consequences.

3. Be very careful how you get out.

Too often, in its Middle East policies, the U.S. has violated all three of these rules.

As the U.S. has contemplated interventions in the Middle East, policy makers have failed to take into account the culture, tribal relationships, ethnic rivalries and the role of religion in the region. Following 9/11, the George W. Bush administration demanded that the Taliban in Afghanistan turn over Osama bin Laden. While recommending that bin Laden leave the country, the Taliban refused to turn him over until they were provided with proof that bin Laden had been involved in the 9/11 attacks. The Bush administration refused to negotiate and attacked Afghanistan in order to overthrow the Taliban. This costly decade-long war may have been avoided if U.S. decision makers had understood *Pashtunwali* (literally "the Pashtun way").

Pashtunwali is the unwritten tribal code that is followed by the Pashtun tribal people of Afghanistan and Pakistan. Among the 10 principles of the code is the concept of "asylum." Asylum to Pashtun people means the protection given to a person against his or her enemies. People are protected at all costs; even those running from the law must be given refuge until the situation can be clarified. Had the Bush administration considered *Pashtunwali* and provided the Taliban with the evidence that they had of bin Laden's involvement, it is likely that he would have been turned over or forced out. Had the Bush administration considered the ethnic and religious divisions in Iraq that had been suppressed under the brutal regime of Saddam Hussein, they might have had second thoughts about a nation-building project.

While unintended consequences of an action are difficult to predict with any certainty, the possible consequences in many cases have been relatively self-evident. Even before the 2003 invasion of Iraq, which had been designed to overthrow the regime of Saddam Hussein and create a democracy in Iraq, it should have been seen that the likely outcome would be a Shia-led government. In a region where religion has long been the organizing principle, Shia majority country elections were almost certain to create a Shia government friendly to Shia Iran. The only winner in the Iraq War was Iran.

Muammar Gaddafi was a Libyan revolutionary and politician, and the de facto ruler of Libya for 42 years.

In many cases, unintended consequences result from a failure to consider the difficulties of getting out of an intervention. In March 2011, in response to a UN resolution to protect civilians, a NATO-led coalition intervened in Libya against the forces of Libyan leader **Muammar Gaddafi**. The operation quickly morphed into an effort to overthrow Gaddafi and his government. Within six months, Gaddafi was overthrown and in October he was captured and killed by rebel militias. The NATO coalition immediately declared victory and headed home. They left behind a dysfunctional government, numerous independent militias and an arsenal of high-tech weaponry such as surface-to-air missiles. The weapons soon spread around the Middle East and North Africa to arm rebels in Syria, Egypt and Mali. The Tuareg tribal members from Mali, who had fought for Gaddafi, returned home to begin an insurrection against the Malian government. Intervening to overthrow a government and then leaving behind chaos is not a recipe for stability.

How We Got Here:

Support for the Axis of Evil (Blog from 1/11/2008)

Many ordinary Iranians that I talked to during my visit to Iran in 2007 expressed the point of view that all of the U.S. saber rattling and "axis of evil" and "regime change" rhetoric was actually helping to keep the unpopular hardline regime in power. Iranians are very proud of their country with its long history and ancient culture and are very patriotic. Anytime their country has been threatened they have rallied around their government no matter how unpopular that government might be. In 1980, for example, Iraq's Saddam Hussein, with the support of the U.S. and other western countries, invaded Iran. At that time, shortly after the Iranian revolution and the founding of the Islamic Republic of Iran, it was unclear which political faction was going to come out on top. The Islamists associated with revolutionary hero Ayatollah Khomeini clearly had the upper hand as they were the best organized, but a number of other factions were jockeying for position. The MEK/MKO (Mujahedin-e Khalq Organization), with its odd Marxist/Islamist ideology, the Communists, the secularists and the monarchists were all players. When Saddam thought that he could take advantage of this factionalism and take over the Iranian oil fields, Iranians of all stripes rallied to the Islamist government and drove out the invader, albeit at the cost of over a million lives on both sides. This phenomenon has been evident in Iran in the past few years.

Mahmoud Ahmadinejad is an Iranian politician who was the sixth President of Iran from 2005 to 2013. He was also the main political leader of the Alliance of Builders of Islamic Iran, a coalition of conservative political groups in the country.

As the U.S./Israel have threatened economic and military action against Iran, the reformist and moderate hardline groups have been reluctant to speak out against the very hardline regime of President **Mahmoud Ahmadinejad**. Opposition leaders have been unwilling to appear unpatriotic and have kept a low profile. The situation appears to have changed somewhat in the past few weeks since the release of the National Intelligence Estimate that downgraded the threat of the Iranian nuclear enrichment program. Most people in the Middle East, whether Arab or Persian, breathed a big sigh of relief and concluded that U.S./Israel would not be able to sustain a consensus for an attack on Iran.

The aggressive rhetoric has subsided somewhat and there are even conversations about having talks. This has given the opposition factions space to escalate their criticism of Ahmadinejad's performance both in foreign affairs and economics. Much of this criticism could not have happened without the tacit approval of the Supreme Leader, Ayatollah Khamenei. This political space is important since, with parliamentary elections imminent, a start could be made toward the installation of a more moderate regime through the democratic process. President Ahmadinejad must be saying to himself, "Where is George Bush when I need him?" Never fear, George is here! The announced primary purpose of Bush's Middle East trip is to ensure that everyone in the region understands the "grave threat" of Iran and to rally the "moderate" Arab states in opposition to Iran. The recent altercation between U.S. warships and Iranian patrol boats in the Strait of Hormuz has been another opportunity for "over the top" rhetoric. This altercation has turned into a battle of videos similar to the battle of GPSs between Iran and the British over the kidnapping, capture, detention or whatever of 15 British sailors and marines last spring. I have reviewed both the U.S. and Iranian videos and agree with the Iranian position that this is a normal course of events in this crowded narrow waterway. It did not appear to rise to the level of a "provocative act" and justify the threat of "serious consequences." However, with hardliners in charge in both countries, it appears that the two leaders are kindred spirits and need each other's support to maintain their positions of power.

More Strange Bed Fellows (Blog from 7/10/2007)

The Middle East is a part of the world where many odd alliances appear. One is never sure who is allied with whom and whatever one thinks may all change tomorrow. After George Bush's State of the Union speech in which he declared Iran part of the "Axis of Evil" and after the well-documented Department of Defense plans for war with Iran, it became clear that the U.S. government considered Iran an archenemy. Ongoing saber rattling and deployment of forces were designed to intimidate the Iranian government. We now seem to have a new ally in our efforts to intimidate Iran and perhaps an ally in any war effort with the Islamic Republic. Our old friends at al-Qaeda also have decided that Iran is an enemy. They have declared that unless Iran ceases its support for the Iraqi government they will begin attacks against Iran. We should, however, think about the unintended consequences of supporting the objectives of al-Qaeda in the Middle East.

The Libya Mess (Blog from 3/22/2011)

As the military intervention in Libya by the "coalition of the willing" led by Britain, France and the U.S. moves toward its second week, all of the divisive issues inherent in such an adventure are starting to appear. The support (however tepid) from the Arab League and the UN Security Council, which was garnered through diplomatic groundwork by the U.S. and its western allies, is starting to splinter. This was eminently predictable as no amount of war planning survives the first contact with the enemy.

The Obama administration was clearly reluctant to resort to military intervention in support of the rebel factions allied against Muammar Gaddafi and his regime. They were wrestling with legitimate and difficult questions including: 1) the availability of resources, 2) the reaction of the Arab and Islamic world to another western attack on an Arab/Muslim country, 3) the effectiveness of a "no-fly zone" and 4) the possibility that even a successful military campaign could result in a negative political outcome. In Washington the political pressure to "do something" (in this case fanned by the same neo-conservative hawks who got us into the Iraq mess) is intense. Faced with this growing pressure Obama decided to move forward with the military option.

As the initial "shock and awe" campaign rapidly evolves into a stalemate, the four questions, so far unanswered, still remain. The U.S. is attempting to resolve the resource problem by rapidly turning the lead responsibility over to Britain and France. They, however, have grown used to the U.S. bailing them out and are quickly getting cold feet. As civilian casualties (real and manufactured) are mounting, the Arab and Muslim support is fading.

The "no-fly zone" appears to have hampered Gaddafi's military capability and reenergized the rebels allowing them to make up some lost ground. There is no sign, however, that they will be able to defeat Gaddafi's forces and drive him from power if he is determined to remain. Absent the coalition committing substantial ground forces to the conflict, it appears that we are in for a long ugly mess.

One possibility for resolving this is to persuade Gaddafi that he has stolen enough money from the Libyan people and can go off to a comfortable retirement. But even this outcome is problematic as Gaddafi has destroyed all Libyan civil society and will leave behind no institutions capable of filling the power vacuum. As a result, all of the tribal, sectarian and ethnic rivalries will come to the surface.

As the Obama administration considered policy options it forgot, or chose to ignore, the fact is that these interventions are a lot easier to get into than they are to get out of.

Mission Creep (Blog from 4/2/2011)

As the Libyan uprising against the regime of Muammar Gaddafi enters its sixth week and the military intervention by the U.S. and its allies enters its third week, the inevitable "mission creep" that is so typical of this kind of operation is becoming more and more evident. What started out as a peaceful uprising by the oppressed people of Libya has deteriorated into a brutal civil war between ragtag groups of armed young rebels against the largely mercenary army loyal to Gaddafi.

Responding to Gaddafi's rants about massacring all who opposed him, the UN Security Council passed resolutions 1970 and 1973 authorizing, among other things, an arms embargo, a "no-fly zone," and military action as necessary to enforce it. The language is clear:

The UNSC *"decides to establish a ban on all flights in the airspace of the Libyan Arab Jamahiriya in order to help protect civilians."*

The UNSC *"authorizes Member States...to take all necessary measures to enforce compliance with the ban on flights."*

The "coalition of the willing," however, quickly realized that a "no-fly zone" was not going to protect civilians and unilaterally declared a "no drive zone" that allowed them to attack Gaddafi's tanks and vehicles. This step also has become problematic. Today a coalition aircraft mistakenly attacked rebel vehicles killing at least seven rebel fighters. (All white pickup trucks look the same from the air.) It is becoming clear that for coalition aircraft to provide effective close air support to the rebels, ground observers are required. Although President Obama has said that he has no intention of putting "American boots on the ground," he already has deployed CIA operatives to coordinate with the rebels and provide targeting information for allied aircraft.

Discussion has now begun about the wisdom of arming and resupplying the rebel forces. The language of UNSC Res. 1970 clearly bans such action. The language here is also straight forward.

The UNSC "*decides that all Member States shall immediately take the necessary measures to prevent the direct or indirect supply, sale or transfer to the Libyan Arab Jamahiriya, from or through their territories or by their nationals, or using their flag vessels or aircraft, or arms and related material of all types...*"

Any violation of this prohibition by the U.S. and its allies would fracture the alliance and make the military mission a U.S. and European action.

What few have acknowledged is that in order to protect civilians, Gaddafi must go. President Obama has specifically ruled out regime change and overthrowing the regime by force. The only way out of this morass is a political solution in which Gaddafi and his cronies choose to leave. And, it needs to happen sooner rather than later.

As British Prime Minister David Cameron and French President Nicolas Sarkozy take a victory lap in Libya, it may be premature to declare such a win. The number of nations that that have formally recognized the Transitional National Council (TNC) as the legitimate government of Libya grows every day. Mustafa Abdul Jalil, the chairman of the TNC, presents a moderate face to the world that plays well in the western media. Behind the scenes of moderation and unity there are many unresolved issues that will be difficult for even the best-intentioned leaders to address.

In contrast with Tunisia and Egypt where the revolutions were largely peaceful and where institutions such as political parties, NGOs, labor unions, etc. were in place, Libya's revolution was protracted and violent and civil society institutions had been destroyed by Gaddafi. There are, therefore, few building blocks upon which to construct a new government structure.

We already are seeing all the societal divisions, which had been suppressed under Gaddafi, reappear within the TNC. The most visible division is between the Islamists and the secularists. Under Gaddafi the secular elites have been the most prominent both within Libya and in the exile community. However, during the revolution, the Islamists have commanded the bulk of the fighters and the weapons. The Islamist forces are the most experienced fighters who fought in Afghanistan, Chechnya, Iraq and the Balkans. They, therefore, have assumed leadership positions. Abdul Jalil of the TNC has attempted to bridge these divides by calling for a moderate Islamic regime with a legal system based on Sharia. Within the TNC there is also rivalry between the Benghazi and Tripoli factions.

The TNC, however, is not completely in charge. Gaddafi is gone, but where is unclear. Many of his supporters have fled across the southern deserts to Niger and Chad. Will they now become the insurgents? Most of the focus has been on the populous coastal region. The huge sparsely populated desert regions of the south have long been havens for bandits and militias. It will now be an ideal place from which an insurgency of Gaddafi loyalists can operate.

Tribal factions are also competing for power and influence. Local tribal militias with no allegiance to the TNC captured many cities from Gaddafi's forces. These armed groups will need to be integrated into the new government structure.

Many of Gaddafi's weapons stockpiles have disappeared. These included not only light weapons and machine guns, but also surface-to-air missiles. With al-Qaeda in the Islamic Maghreb (AQIM) right across the porous border with Algeria, this raises the threat of attacks on passenger planes.

President Obama was wise to allow the British and French to be the face of the NATO operations and to avoid a premature "mission accomplished moment." Obama said at the onset of hostilities, "Libya is not Iraq." It does, however, look a lot like Afghanistan.

The Syrian Dilemma (Blog from 11/22/2011)

One question I am frequently asked is, "What is the U.S. policy in Syria and why are we acting differently in Syria than we did in Libya?" In considering these questions I am reminded of the words of a Middle East expert who, when asked about U.S. Middle East policy, responded, "We don't have a policy in the Middle East, but that's just as well because, if we did, it would be the wrong one." Before discussing Syria, examine the Libyan situation.

The Brotherly Leader of Libya, Gaddafi, was an easy target for international military support for a revolution. In addition to his eccentric antics, he had managed, through his words and policies over the years, to make enemies of nearly everybody—the western powers, fellow Arab leaders (especially in the wealthy, autocratic Gulf States) and his own people. When the western powers, following the approval of UN Resolution 1973 authorizing "all necessary actions to protect civilians," and while interpreting the resolution very liberally, embarked on a policy of regime change, no one came to Gaddafi's defense. The situation in Syria is quite different.

While Libya was isolated politically, diplomatically and geographically, Syria sits in the middle of the volatile Levant region bordering Iraq, Lebanon, Turkey, Jordan and Israel. It is a major player in the so-called "axis of resistance" along with Iran, Hezbollah and Hamas. Any western intervention in Syria would likely bring Assad's allies into the conflict with serious regional consequences.

The divisions in Libyan society are largely tribal in nature. On the other hand, in Syria, tribal rivalries are overlaid with sectarian divisions. The Christian and Alawite (an offshoot of Shia Islam) minorities are generally part of and supportive of the regime, whereas the majority Sunni Muslims see themselves as oppressed.

Faced with these complicating factors, an overriding concern about the rise of Iran and a possible threat to Israel, the U.S. is attempting to create its own version of the *Great Game* between Russia and Britain

The **Gulf States** refer to the Arab states bordering the Persian Gulf, namely Kuwait, Iraq, Bahrain, Oman, Qatar, Saudi Arabia and the United Arab Emirates (UAE). Most of these nations are part of the Cooperation Council for the Arab States of the Gulf (formerly the Gulf Cooperation Council, GCC).

Salafists are those in Sunni Islam who advocate a literal, strict and puritanical approach to Islam as practiced by the earliest Muslims in the 7th century.

in Central Asia in the 19th Century. The U.S. is attempting to mobilize and co-opt regional players such as Turkey, Qatar, Saudi Arabia and the UAE, to confront the resistance axis and orchestrate regime change in Syria. This effort, well financed by the wealthy **Gulf States,** appears to be turning the uprising against the Assad regime into a low-grade civil war.

The conservative Gulf monarchies have long despised the secular Assad regime in Syria. Among their Sunni proxies in Syria are a large number of **Salafist** groups including many jihadist fighters who were kicked out of Iraq and who have set up shop in Syria. Orchestrating a Syria/Iran conflict as part of the effort to remake the *New Middle East*, while utilizing allies with different agendas, is risky business and may come back to haunt the U.S. and its allies.

Syria's Budding Civil War (Blog from 4/4/2012)

In the middle of the last decade, during the dark days of internecine violence in Iraq following the 2003 U.S. invasion, there was a vociferous political argument as to whether or not there was *civil war* in Iraq. As with many political debates in the U.S., the discussion was generally devoid of facts and intellectual rigor. No one bothered to define exactly what constitutes a *civil war*. Scholars generally describe a civil war as a violent conflict within the recognized borders of a state whose participants are geographically contiguous and concerned with having to live with one another after the conflict. Both sides must have formally organized armed forces and must control some amount of territory. The purpose of this definition is to differentiate *civil war* from other domestic violence such as riots and guerrilla insurgencies.

By this definition the year-long Syrian uprising seems to be morphing into a civil war. The members of the so-called "Friends of Syria" (FOS) group led by the U.S. and its allies have recognized the Syrian National Council (SNC) as the legitimate representative of the Syrian opposition and promised to provide support to the Free Syrian Army (FSA). The conservative Sunni Gulf State monarchies, led by Qatar, have gone farther by declaring their intent to support the Syrian opposition against the Shia Assad regime "by all means," including supplying weapons and paying the FSA. Ironically, this has put the FOS on the same side as al-Qaeda, which has declared its support for the Syrian uprising. Support from al-Qaeda has brought an increase in the flow of experienced jihadist fighters from Lebanon, Iraq and Libya into the FSA.

One characteristic of civil wars is, once they begin, they are notoriously difficult to end. Ending an interstate war is hard enough, but in that case, one side will eventually return to its own territory and the war will end. In civil wars, where partition is not possible (as in the case of Syria), the two sides who have been killing each other must either live side by side and work together peacefully in a common government or one side must be victorious and get all. In order for the war to end, both sides must be simultaneously pessimistic about the possibility of improving their situation by continuing fighting. The prospect of outside intervention only increases the likelihood that one side or the other will conclude that if it only fights on a little longer, its position will improve. In an internal conflict, stalemate is an acceptable alternative to losing.

As the outside forces, FOS on one side and Russia, China and Iran on the other, escalate their support for their preferred party, the prospect for Syria is years of violence, bloodshed and instability. The duration of post WWII civil wars is usually measured in decades and the wars usually do not end, but merely become frozen conflicts or guerrilla insurgencies.

The Syrian Dilemma, Part 2 (Blog from 1/23/2012)

After months of opposition demonstrations, counter demonstrations by regime supporters, attacks on opposition demonstrators by government forces, terrorist bombings of government facilities, various efforts at international intervention, charges and counter charges, the situation in Syria is, in a word, a "mess." Currently there are three wars going on in this strategically located, but fragile, state: 1) There is a low-grade civil war between government and opposition forces. 2) There is a proxy war between the U.S., supported by its Gulf State and European allies, and Iran, supported by its ally Hezbollah. And, finally, 3) there is a war of perceptions in which facts are the first casualty.

The U.S. and its supporters in the conservative Sunni Gulf States, particularly Qatar and the UAE, would like to see regime change in Syria and Iran and a weakening of the Shia resistance group Hezbollah. Under Secretary of State for the Near East, Jeffrey Feltman, while describing U.S. regime change policy in Syria, said that the U.S. would "relentlessly pursue our two-track strategy of supporting the opposition and diplomatically and financially strangling the regime until that outcome is achieved."

The Arab League has dispatched a monitoring team to Syria in order to attempt to reach a mediated solution. Qatar and the Istanbul-based opposition Syrian National Council (SNC), on the other hand, have criticized the Arab League mission and have pushed for western military intervention rather than a mediated solution that would reform the regime, but leave Assad in power.

The western media have portrayed the Syrian situation as one in which a peaceful opposition, representing the overwhelming majority of Syrians, is faced off against a brutal, intransigent regime. However, a recent poll conducted by the Qatar-based Doha Debates points out that while 81 percent of Arabs want President Assad to step down, 55 percent of Syrians are supportive of Assad and do not want Assad to resign. The respondents said that without Assad, they feared for the future of their country.

The appalling statistics of massacres, rapes of Sunni women and girls and torture by regime supporters that have been reported by the western media with the disclaimer "we were unable to confirm the accuracy of these figures" have been largely provided by the British-based Syrian National Observatory (SNO). The SNO is an arm of the SNC and is funded by a Dubai-based pooled fund of western and Gulf money and thus the accuracy of these figures is suspect. Somehow the media has not managed to receive reports of casualties among regime supporters and military forces.

The U.S.-based private intelligence group, Stratfor, has advised caution on the accuracy of the mainstream narrative on Syria saying, "With two sides to every war...the war of perceptions in Syria is no exception."

Questions and Answers on Syria (Blog from 9/8/2013)

When the Obama administration began its march toward war with Syria last month, there were numerous questions that were begging for answers. During the weeks of debate, posturing and political maneuvering that have followed, some answers have become more clear and some remain obscured. The initial question for me was, "What is the evidence that the chemical attack in the suburbs of Damascus was perpetrated by the Assad government?" Secretary of State John Kerry has tried to make the case that the links to Assad are undeniable, but no evidence has been produced to substantiate this claim. There are plenty of reasons to be skeptical of the carefully worded unclassified Intelligence Estimate often cited in support of the war, which seems more designed to obscure the facts than to elucidate them. We are being asked to accept the administration's judgment on faith. After the Iraq fiasco, this is not something I am quick to do. Acceptance is especially difficult since administration officials have told media outlets that the evidence is not a "slam-dunk."

A second question is, "What are the strategic outcomes that the administration intends to achieve?" This question has had many answers depending on who is answering, when and to whom they are speaking. The answers cover a broad ground; limited strikes to punish the regime, targeted strikes to degrade the regime's capabilities, strikes intended to shift the military balance and bring the parties to the negotiating table, regime change, to send a message to Iran, to weaken Iran and Hezbollah in order to protect Israel, to uphold U.S. credibility (whatever that means) and prevent a political defeat for Obama. The list grows longer by the day. It is, therefore, not surprising that, in a rare moment of candor, when asked by Senator Bob Corker about the administration's strategic objectives, Joint Chiefs Chairman Martin Dempsey replied, "I can't answer that question."

The answer to the question, "How has the U.S. prepared to deal with the unintended consequences of war with Syria?" is even less clear. These consequences are numerous. Al Akhbar reports, "Informed *insiders* have confirmed that Syria and Hezbollah plan to retaliate against Israel in the event of an American-led military attack on Syria. Says one, 'If even one U.S. missile hits Syria, we will take this battle to Israel.'" If the attacks turn the tide of the civil war, will Iran intervene to aid Assad? If the rebels carry the day and begin a raft of revenge killings, how will the U.S. respond? Russia has moved warships to the eastern Mediterranean. How will they respond? U.S. intelligence has claimed that, in the event of an attack, Iran has instructed its allies in Iraq and Lebanon to strike at U.S. targets. If the Assad regime loses control of chemical and biological weapons to the al-Qaeda linked rebels, how will the U.S. respond? There is no mood in Russia, China or Iran to give the U.S. an easy win. It is instructive of the administration position, that, again in a rare moment of candor, Secretary of State John Kerry responding to a question about the usefulness of a ban on the use of ground troops in the Senate war resolution, said, "I don't want to take off the table an option that might or might not be available to a president of the United States to secure our country."

As former British intelligence officer Alastair Crooke points out in his always insightful commentary, "The precise consequences from lobbing cruise missiles can never be foreseen, and although always, before the event, such interventions are assumed to be quick and painless, it seldom turns out that way in practice."

Unintended Consequences of Obama's ISIS Plan
(Blog from 9/24/2014)

Over the last two weeks, the U.S. has begun an air campaign in Iraq and Syria, bombing ISIS ammunition inventories, carrying out targeted killings of ISIS leaders, destroying military equipment that ISIS has captured from the Iraqi military, blowing up oil refineries— all in an effort to degrade the capability of ISIS or the Islamic State (IS). This tactic, seeming to have short-term success, carries substantial risk of unintended consequences that could pose a greater threat to U.S. security than that presented by the current Islamic State.

This is not the first intervention in the history of U.S. involvement in the Middle East that has resulted in unintended consequences that have "come home to roost." The most egregious example is the arming, financing and training of the Mujahideen to fight the Soviet Union in Afghanistan, which eventually resulted in the 9/11 attacks. Another example is the U.S.-led overthrow of Libya's Muammar Gaddafi, which empowered and strengthened al-Qaeda in North Africa, resulting in growing chaos and instability throughout the region.

Ever since his September 8 announcement of the U.S. plan to "degrade and destroy" ISIS, President Obama has done little to explain exactly what "degrade and destroy" means in terms of a strategic goal and the tactics that will be used to achieve it. The tactics that seem to be emerging are a combination of air strikes in Syria and Iraq, designed to harass ISIS forces, and an effort to train and equip the Iraqi Army, Kurdish Peshmerga and so-called moderate rebel groups in Syria to bear the brunt of the ground combat necessary to dislodge ISIS from the territory that it has conquered in eastern Syria and Central Western Iraq. As Obama has pointed out, the program to train these regional fighters is a long-term project and, in my opinion, given the failure of the multi-year, multi-billion dollar effort to train the Iraqi Army following the invasion of Iraq, has dubious prospects for success. However, the prospects for unintended consequences from the aerial harassment campaign are great:

1. The blowback from civilian collateral damage from the air strikes, which are based on limited intelligence, is certain to incentivize ISIS to attack the far enemy, the U.S., rather than concentrating its efforts on maintaining a grip on the conquered territory. In early air strikes the United Kingdom-based Syrian Observatory for Human Rights reports that eight civilians including three children have

been killed. All of these have brothers, sisters, friends and fellow tribe members who are now very angry with the U.S. Some may actually live in the U.S. Already the Department of Homeland Security has warned of security threats originating in Syria. Aleppo-based al-Monitor correspondent, Edward Dark, (a pseudonym) reports, "It would be foolish to believe that U.S. military action against IS is popular here or will go down well, especially when civilian casualties start to mount. On the contrary, it will most likely prove counterproductive, stoking anti-Western resentment among the population and increasing support for IS, driving even more recruits to its ranks. The terror group knows this well, which is why it is secretly overjoyed at the prospect of military action against it. In its calculations, the loss of fighters to strikes is more than outweighed by the outpouring of support it expects both locally and on the international jihadist scene."

2. Because the harassment campaign will not dislodge ISIS from the territory that it controls, the nation states of Syria and Iraq as we have known them since shortly after World War I will disappear. While the final outcome of the campaign to degrade ISIS is unclear, the most likely result is the creation of rump states in western and southern Syria controlled by the Syrian government of Bashar al-Assad, a Shiite-controlled Iraqi state in southern Iraq, a Kurdish-controlled rump state in northern Iraq and either a chaotic or ISIS-controlled state in eastern Syria and central/western Iraq. Statements by Iranian President Hassan Rouhani that, "Baghdad and the holy sites (in Karbala) are a red line for Iran" seem to indicate that Iran is okay with the breakup of Iraq as long as it doesn't infringe on Iran and the Iraqi Shiite population. An outcome that leaves ISIS in control, however tenuously, does not seem to be a recipe for stability.

Unless the Obama administration is able to find a way to put "boots on the ground" sufficient to restore the status quo ante—an unlikely prospect given its poor relations with the most powerful players, Iran, Turkey and Syria—the probable outcome is a drastically altered map of the Middle East. Since the U.S. cannot prevent the unintended consequences, the key to dealing with this situation is to recognize and deal with the down sides.

CHAPTER 7
Conflicting Goals

As the U.S. government has attempted to craft policies in support of its national interests, it has become apparent that, at times, the interests are conflicting, if not mutually exclusive. Since the founding of the State of Israel as a "homeland for the Jews," America's uncritical support for Israel has been a major obstacle to U.S. efforts to improve relations with oil-producing Arab states. The Arab governments and elites may, at times, have supported U.S. policies, but this support has never reflected the views of ordinary citizens. Whenever Arab governments have considered the views of their citizens, their governments have not supported U.S. policies. American policymakers, endeavoring to maintain a stable oil market while uncritically supporting Israel, have found these policies to be difficult to reconcile. The contradiction has been a driving force in America's involvement in the Israel-Palestine issue and its episodic efforts to help craft an Israel-Palestine peace agreement. Domestic political considerations have complicated these efforts and have prevented the U.S. from functioning as an unbiased broker in negotiations. America's unswerving political and military support for Israel has impaired any influence it might have had on Israel's behavior and negotiating position. U.S.-led negotiations historically have been unproductive and the failures have frequently led to outbreaks of violent resistance, all the while undermining America's efforts to maintain stability.

The United States also exhibited conflicting goals throughout the Cold War. America's desire to prevent the Soviet Union from exerting influence led the U.S. to back unsavory regimes such as that of the Shah of Iran. Iranian resentment of U.S. support for a brutal dictator brought an anti-American government to power after the Iranian Revolution. The U.S. recruited and supported an army of radical Sunni jihadists in its proxy war with the Soviet Union in Afghanistan, which was designed to mitigate Soviet threats to Middle East oil supplies. The jihadists eventually formed the core of al-Qaeda and the Taliban. In more recent times, Iran has succeeded the Soviet Union as the regional "boogie man." So, in an effort to contain Iranian influence, the U.S. has supported jihadist groups engaged in the Syrian civil war. These groups eventually formed the core of ISIS.

As the U.S. has attempted to balance its desire for stability with promotion of democracy, it has made no one happy. While supporting Egypt's democracy revolution in 2011, the U.S. maintained ties with Saudi Arabia, which is an undemocratic autocracy and which intervened militarily in Bahrain in order to suppress Bahraini democracy activists. When the Egyptian military, with the backing of Saudi Arabia, orchestrated a coup to overthrow the democratically elected Egyptian government of **Mohamed Morsi,** the U.S. refused to condemn the coup. The *Wall Street Journal* pointed out, "The Obama administration's refusal to publicly condemn the Egyptian military's threat to intervene in Cairo's political crisis fueled the belief—both in the Middle East and Washington—that the U.S. tacitly supports a coup against President Mohamed Morsi. The view conflicts with another of the many conspiracy theories held among many Egyptians in the opposition: that the Obama administration has a secret pact with Mr. Morsi to support ... (the Muslim Brotherhood)."[20]

> **Mohamed Morsi** is an Egyptian politician who served as the fifth president of Egypt, from June 30, 2012 to July 3, 2013. He was the first democratically elected head of state in Egyptian history. He was overthrown, arrested and imprisoned in July 2013 as the result of a military coup led by General Abdel El-Sisi.

In Syria, as the demonstrations against the al-Assad government were becoming more widespread and the government response was becoming more brutal, the U.S. was faced with a dilemma. One option was to take diplomatic steps in conjunction with Russia, Iran and Saudi Arabia to try to stem the violence and prevent the conflict from becoming a full-blown Civil War. This would have required compromises on all sides and likely would have left the Assad government in power. The second option was to take the rigid position that "Assad must go" and support the opposition forces, hoping that the Assad government could be overthrown.

Option one, if successful, would bring the violence to an end, but would have left the Assad government in place. Option two, if successful, would, hopefully, have resulted in a Syrian government more accommodating to U.S. and Israeli interests. By reducing arms supplies between Iran and its ally Hezbollah in Lebanon, the new arrangement would reduce the Hezbollah threat to Israel. The U.S. tried to accomplish both objectives at once: arming and supporting the opposition with advisers while, at the same time, convening peace conferences in order to end the conflict. As is usually the case, neither objective was accomplished.

How We Got Here:

More Conflicting Conflicts (Blog from 10/29/2007)

Since World War II, the United States' strategic policies regarding the Middle East have been either in conflict or completely opposed to one another. Some would argue that "strategic" and "U.S. Middle East policy" are not words that should be used in the same sentence. I have maintained that Osama bin Laden has an advantage in his conflict with the U.S. since he has an established strategy whereas the U.S. is completely focused on tactics. The U.S. has even declared war on a tactic, the so-called "war on terror." After 1945, America's primary objectives in the region were securing Western access to Middle Eastern oil, preventing the Soviet Union from reaping political or strategic advantage in the area, and ensuring Israel's security. However, by pursuing the last of these objectives, ensuring Israel's security, the pursuit of the other two became complicated. Washington's close relations with Israel generated anti-American sentiment in the Arab world, providing the Soviet Union with opportunities to increase its political influence in the region. Similarly, during the Yom Kippur War of 1973, President Richard M. Nixon's decision to airlift military supplies to Israel prompted oil-producing Arab states to impose an embargo on oil shipments to the United States and some European countries, causing major dislocations in the global economy.

As the Cold War drew to an end, the imperative of containing the Soviet Union gave way to two new objectives: combating international terrorism and preventing so called "rogue" states—such as Libya, Iran, and Iraq—from challenging U.S. policies in the region. Both of these objectives have acquired fresh urgency following the terrorist attacks of September 11, 2001, but Americans disagree over whether the two goals can, or should, be pursued simultaneously. While former President George W. Bush argued that the necessity of disarming Iraq, and overthrowing its government as well, could not be separated from the effort to defeat Osama bin Laden's al-Qaeda network, others insist that Bush's preoccupation with Iraq has diverted precious energy and resources from the war against al-Qaeda.

As in previous decades, Washington continues to be unable to secure any formula for pursuing its diverse objectives in the Middle East. The U.S. objectives in the region are to contain and disrupt Iranian influence, to support the Kurdish regional government in Iraq as a poster child for positive results from the U.S. invasion, and to occupy and cultivate good relations with Turkey as a moderate Islamic state, a bridge to the Middle East and a conduit for oil and natural gas flow to the west. In order to help accomplish the first objective, the U.S. has supported and armed the Kurdish Workers' Party (PKK) and their affiliate, the PJAK, in their attacks on Iran. This has created the problem that the PKK has used this support and arms to attack Turkey. After numerous deadly cross border raids Turkey has asked the Iraqi central government, the U.S., and the Kurdish regional government to crack down on PKK bases in Iraq and to prevent the attacks across the border. The Iraqi government has no ability to accomplish this as they have limited resources and those that they do have are not allowed to operate in Kurdish areas. The U.S. is unwilling to do anything because it supports the PKK attacks on Iran and is reluctant to risk destabilizing the only part of Iraq that shows any signs of progress. The Kurdish regional government has no desire to do anything because its long-range objective is an independent greater Kurdistan incorporating the Kurdish areas of Iraq, Turkey, Syria and Iran. The result of all this is that our erstwhile ally, Turkey, and our erstwhile enemy, Iran, are meeting to discuss how to work together to solve their common problem.

The "Arab Spring" Brings Policy Challenges for the U.S. (Blog from 5/3/2011)

As the pro-democracy uprisings have spread across the Middle East and North Africa, sweeping from power U.S.-supported authoritarian regimes in Tunisia and Egypt and threatening other regimes, U.S. policy makers are facing a number of new challenges. The U.S. is learning that the new governments coming to power reflect the views of their citizens who generally are not as supportive of U.S. policies as previous regimes.

For several years, the U.S. has expressed tepid support for efforts by Egypt under Hosni Mubarak and his intelligence chief Omar Suleiman to achieve reconciliation between the rival Palestinian Hamas and Fatah factions. This effort was never successful because Egypt was never an "honest broker" and never genuinely wanted reconciliation. Mubarak was afraid of a successful Palestinian government in which Hamas (an offshoot of the Egyptian Muslim Brotherhood) participated, as it would inspire Egypt's Muslim Brotherhood opposition. The U.S. and Israel were perfectly happy with the status quo that divided the Palestinians.

It didn't take long for the new Egyptian government to change the landscape. After several weeks of secret negotiations, the parties announced a reconciliation agreement, which is to be signed on Wednesday. Most observers, myself included, felt that the new Egyptian government, which includes the Muslim Brotherhood, would change the negotiating dynamic. What did surprise me, however, is how fast the agreement happened. While it is still possible that the agreement will fall apart over details of implementation, so far, it appears to be on track.

A Palestinian unity government with Hamas as a participant creates big policy dilemmas for both the U.S. and Israel. Israel has immediately condemned the agreement, called on Fatah to back out and stopped transfer of tax revenues, which they collect for the

Palestinian Authority (PA). The U.S. has issued its pro-forma statement calling Hamas a terrorist organization and repeating its well-worn preconditions.

There are several possible outcomes to this state of affairs. One is that the U.S. and Israel will succeed in pressuring the PA and Egypt to abandon the deal. While possible, it seems unlikely, as Egypt has already announced that it will completely open the Rafah border crossing into Gaza. Another, although unlikely, outcome is that the U.S. will recognize that Hamas is an essential player in any agreement and deal with the unity government. The most likely outcome is that Israel and the U.S. Congress will cut off all tax and aid payments to the PA. The result of the cutoff of aid will either be a collapse of the PA or some other entity filling the gap.

The collapse of the PA would not be all bad as it would throw the whole mess back on the Israelis, further straining their resources. Iran is a good candidate for filling the breach, as it would further enhance their influence. It is unlikely that Saudi Arabia would allow Iran to accomplish this and, therefore, they will be forced to back the PA. Whatever the outcome, the U.S. influence in the region will decline even further.

The Changing Face of the GCC (Blog from 5/18/2011)

The Gulf Cooperation Council (GCC) was founded in 1981 as a cultural and economic union of six Persian Gulf states: Bahrain, United Arab Emirates, Saudi Arabia, Kuwait, Oman and Qatar. The founding purposes of the group were economic integration and cooperation, defense cooperation, and strengthened private sector cooperation, which were similar to those of the European Economic Community and its successor the European Union. The founding countries have much in common culturally, governmentally and economically. They are all Persian Gulf states with small, predominately Sunni Muslim, **Bedouin** indigenous populations. All are relatively wealthy with

Bedouins are Arabic-speaking nomadic people of the Middle Eastern deserts, especially of North Africa, the Arabian Peninsula, Egypt, Israel, Iraq, Syria and Jordan.

large petroleum resources. They are governed by Sunni Muslim absolute monarchs.

The pro-democracy uprisings that have spread across North Africa and the Middle East have completely changed the political landscape in this area. Try as they might, the GCC countries have not been able to immunize themselves from the spreading democracy virus. Oil wealth has allowed leaders the economic flexibility to "buy off" the protestors. (Sultan Qaboos of Oman responded to protests by doubling the minimum wage and creating 50,000 new jobs.) The Sunni al Khalifa ruling family in Bahrain, faced with uprisings led by the majority Shia population, was not as successful in co-opting the demonstrations and the GCC was forced to deploy its joint armed forces (The Peninsula Shield Force) to brutally suppress the pro-democracy movement.

The ruling families in these oil rich sheikdoms are now looking over their shoulders and have started to take action to protect their privileged positions. The GCC has invited Jordan and Morocco to become members. Neither of these countries has oil wealth or geography in common with the founding members. What they do have in common is Sunni absolute monarchies and they have strong western trained military establishments. The GCC is morphing into an association of western oriented Sunni autocrats positioning themselves to confront the so-called "Shia Crescent," Iran and its allies in Iraq, Syria and Lebanon.

The varying outcomes of the pro-democracy uprisings have shown that just having a strong military is not enough to suppress determined demonstrators. In order to succeed, the military must be willing to shoot its own citizens. In Egypt, Hosni Mubarak fell because the military would not shoot their fellow Egyptians. In Bahrain and Libya the non-violent protests failed because the military, largely composed of foreign mercenaries, was willing to shoot. Learning this lesson, the UAE has hired the founder of the American private security firm, Blackwater Worldwide, and other Americans to set up an internal security battalion of foreign troops. Although Blackwater, a major U.S. contractor in Iraq and Afghanistan, has a well-deserved reputation for brutality, the U.S. has supported this project.

Egypt's Messy Politics Get Worse (Blog from 12/8/2012)

Two years ago Tunisia, Egypt and Libya led the way into the so-called "Arab Spring" by successfully ousting long-entrenched authoritarian regimes. Tunisia accomplished this with a relatively peaceful series of demonstrations that forced President Ali to leave. Egypt's overthrow of President Mubarak was more violent, but still relatively peaceful. Libya, on the other hand, endured months of civil war in order to force Muammar Gaddafi from power. I thought at the time that Libya would have the most difficult time in transitioning to a democratic system. Gaddafi had destroyed all of Libya's civil society institutions and the country had a history of sometimes violent tribal rivalries. Despite these problems, Libya has managed a relatively successful transition and the International Monetary Fund (IMF) predicts that the economy will grow at a rate of 116 percent in 2012.

On the other hand, Egypt, the so called "leader of the Arab world," has allowed its political issues to deteriorate into one big street brawl with opposing political groups shooting at each other. In order to understand how we got into this state of affairs, it is useful to examine the history of the Egyptian electoral process and how the various parties read the results differently.

The process began when the Supreme Council of the Armed Forces (SCAF) assumed power following Mubarak's ouster. SCAF decided to hold elections before drafting a new constitution. The rapid time-table for Parliamentary elections favored the more organized Islamist parties. Following a convoluted series of elections and an even more obscure system of allocating seats, the Islamist parties emerged with 65 percent of the votes and 70 percent of the seats. Unsurprisingly, the Constituent Assembly, tasked by Parliament with writing the Constitution, was dominated by Islamists.

The Presidential elections were held in two stages. In the first stage, which determined who would move to the second round, the Muslim Brotherhood (MB) candidate Mohamed Morsi (25 percent) edged out Ahmed Shafik, a remnant (*falool*) of the Mubarak regime (23 percent). The remaining moderate and secular parties could not agree on a common candidate and split the vote resulting in Morsi and Shafik facing off in the second round. In this round Morsi won a narrow victory (52 to 48 percent) with many voters voting against the MB rather than for Shafik. All this said, however, it should be pointed out that, however convoluted the process, Mohamed Morsi is the most democratically elected president in Egypt's history.

The MB looked at the parliamentary results and concluded that they had an overwhelming mandate to govern. This conclusion has led to governing overreach. The opposition, on the other hand, looked at the presidential results and concluded that a majority of Egyptians oppose the MB. The secularist and *falool* parties, who couldn't agree on anything during the elections, have formed an odd coalition, the National Salvation Front (NSF). They have called the "regime" illegitimate, called for its overthrow and vowed that they "will not allow the constitutional referendum to go forward." The tanks are back in the streets again. As Jason Brownlee points out in a recent article, by banking on military intervention and "courting a coup against Morsi or prolonging Egypt's transition (the NSF) risks erasing the great strides made toward popular sovereignty and civilian control over the state." Reza Aslan's Tweet sums it up, "For God's sake, Egypt. The world is watching. Throwing rocks at each other is not politics. Get your shit together!"

King Abdullah's Dilemma (Blog from 5/1/2012)

With the recent resignation of Prime Minister Awn Shawkat Al-Khasawneh after only six months in office, the Jordanian political merry-go-round continued to spin. Ever since the Arab Awakening arrived in Amman last year, King Abdullah has enhanced his strategy of avoiding political reforms by expressing support for reform, appointing study committees, ignoring their recommendations, blaming the failure on the Prime Minister and then firing the Prime Minister. The exiting PM then fades gracefully into the background until called upon again in some future political round. As the International Crisis Group recently reported, "The king has shuffled cabinets and then shuffled them again, using prime ministers as buffers to absorb popular discontent. He has charged committees to explore possible reforms, but these remain largely unimplemented."[21]

Al-Khasawneh violated all the political rules by resigning in a curtly worded letter submitted while he was traveling in Turkey. Al-Khasawneh was generally seen as a reformist, liberal politician determined to root out corruption and rein in the intelligence service. He opened dialogue with the Muslim Brotherhood-affiliated Islamic Action Front and other opposition groups. His failure to deliver on his promises and his introduction of a new election law designed to further marginalize the opposition by banning religious parties and limiting the number of opposition seats in Parliament cost him what support he had among opposition MPs.

The Jordanian political landscape is characterized by sharp divisions between "East Bankers" and "West Bankers." The "East Bankers" are largely Bedouins who tend to vote along tribal lines and generally support the monarch. The "West Bankers" are largely urban Palestinians who migrated to today's Jordan when the West Bank was part of Transjordan or are refugees from the wars of 1948 and 1967. Making up half of Jordan's population, "West Bankers" tend to be more Islamic in their politics and advocate for a more powerful and representative Parliament. Election laws that weigh the tribal vote much more heavily than the urban vote have marginalized them politically.

Low-level unrest demanding real reform and deteriorating economic conditions continue to plague the ruling political class. The new Prime Minister, Fayez Tarawneh, is seen as a conservative who is unlikely to bring about significant change.

When I was in Jordan last month, I asked a number of Jordanians about their views on the current political situation. Most that I spoke with expressed support for King Abdullah and his fashionable wife, Rania. I tend to agree with Middle East analyst Shadi Hamid of the Brookings Institute Doha Center who commented on Twitter, "Jordan will seem 'stable,' until it's not. And then it will be too late."

Egypt's Political Collapse (Blog from 7/8/2013)

Following the ouster of Egypt's democratically elected President Mohamed Morsi by the Egyptian Army and the arrest of many Muslim Brotherhood (MB) leaders and the shuttering of pro-MB media outlets, the Obama administration has struggled to decide how to react to the fast-moving events on the ground. Obama's advisers differ on whether to support the democratically elected government or to back the Egyptian military that has a history of being supportive of U.S. policies in the Middle East. The end result has been a series of bland statements calling for peaceful resolution.

In its effort to formulate a coherent policy, the administration has had no shortage of free advice. *New York Times* columnist David Brooks, in an opinion piece supporting the coup, justified the action by arguing that it overthrew a government that he didn't like.[22]

I also received an email from an Egyptian friend who supported the military's action saying:

> Please explain to all your families and friends and deliver to the media that the Egyptian army is protecting the will of the Egyptians to get rid of the Terrorist Muslim Brotherhood, 33 million Egyptians went out in the streets, our army is protecting us. Morsi is calling for a civil war, we are asking for an early presidential election to stop the deterioration of our country and economy. This man and his group are traitors.

Others have argued that the removal of a democratically elected Islamist government by the military echoes events in Algeria that led to a bloody civil war. The message to political Islam is that you cannot trust democracy. You won't be allowed to win. The message from the Arab Awakening was that al-Qaeda was wrong; an Islamic government can be established through a democratic process. After Egypt, al-Qaeda will say, "I told you so."

I come down on the side that the road to political change in a democracy is through the ballot box and not through confrontation in the street. Sometimes in a democracy, the guy you don't like wins. If you don't like it, change it in the next election. As an Arab friend once said to me, "We can forgive you for electing George W. Bush the first time. Everybody makes mistakes. But the second time, what were you thinking?"

Following today's massacre of over 40 MB supporters by security forces and the defense of it by Egypt's so called "liberals," it is hard to see how this can end happily for Egypt. The choices are stark. Either the military has to cave in and restore Morsi to power (an unlikely event) or the MB has to quietly go away. (Also an unlikely event.) Even quick elections that are free, fair and open are unlikely to heal the huge political divisions in Egypt. The MB would probably win free and fair elections as the opposition is a fractious coalition of Salafists, liberals, and remnants of the Mubarak regime that is already falling apart and probably would not survive the political process. We are then back to square one. This is a sad time for Egypt and its people.

In addition to the negative consequences of the Arab Awakening for the stability of America's long time Middle Eastern allies, the resulting unrest and chaos have created opportunities for America's adversaries.

Egypt: Can Further Collapse Be Prevented?
(Blog from 7/27/2013)

As Egypt rapidly descends into chaos and as the likelihood of a brutal crackdown by the army on disaffected Islamists increases, the U.S. is struggling to find a path forward that is politically palatable and which supports American interests. American national interest has tradition-ally been defined as a stable environment that protects Israel, provides low-cost energy and allows free access to the Suez Canal. In a 2005 speech at American University in Cairo, Secretary of State Condi Rice forcefully articulated a new approach for American policy in the Middle East saying, "The U.S. pursuit of stability in the Middle East at the expense of democracy had achieved neither. Now, we are taking a different course. We are supporting the democratic aspirations of all people." This new approach lasted less than a year. In January 2006, Hamas won a free and fair election in Palestine and the U.S. promptly cut off aid and isolated the Palestinian Authority. Since then, support for democracy has largely taken a back seat to other considerations.

Many have praised the Obama administration's pragmatic approach to the "Arab Awakening." The U.S. has supported democracy move-ments in Tunisia and Egypt and violent revolutions in Libya and Syria, while at the same time supporting brutal suppression of opposition movements in Saudi Arabia and Bahrain. There is, however, a fine line between a pragmatic, tactical approach and having no strategy.

The lack of a strategic approach has led to verbal gymnastics by administration spokespersons in order to avoid calling the Egyptian Army's overthrow of the democratically elected government a coup which would trigger a cut off of aid to the government. While the Morsi government was certainly guilty of incompetence and a majoritarian approach, fortunately for U.S. democracy, these are not fatal sins justifying a coup. As the old saying goes, "If it looks like a duck and quacks like a duck, it is probably a duck." The U.S. government has little ability to influence the outcome in Egypt, but its failure to take any position has alienated all sides.

If the U.S. is to have any ability to prevent Egypt from driving over a cliff, it must make clear to the military that it rejects a return to "Mubarakism without Mubarak" and a return to "emergency law" in the name of the "War on Terror." It must also insist on the release of Muslim Brotherhood leaders, opening of shuttered media outlets and prompt free and fair elections with all parties participating. It must be clear that U.S. military aid depends on their actions.

Conflicting Policy Goals: The Achilles Heel of U.S. Middle East Policy (Blog from 9/17/2014)

U.S. Middle East policy has long been plagued with goals that are contradictory and frequently mutually exclusive. While it is understandable that a global power such as the U.S. would find itself confronted with overlapping interests that do not necessarily match up with regional political realities, the lack of a coherent policy direction in pursuit of vital national interests has hindered the United States' ability to achieve its policy goals and has led to a significant loss of ability to influence regional events. This is not a new phenomenon, but one that has plagued policy makers since the U.S. has attempted to influence events in the Middle East. Recent events in Iraq and Syria have raised this issue to a whole new level of importance, a level that deserves the attention of political leaders.

In the 1950s, the U.S. began to realize that Great Britain and France, drastically weakened by the devastation of World War II, could no longer be the guarantors of regional stability and, thereby, ensure the unfettered flow of the oil required to fuel the post-war economic boom. Efforts to maintain a stable region called for good relations with the oil producing Arab states and minimal conflict within the region. At the same time the conflict between Arab states and the fledgling state of Israel became a major source of instability. Beginning in the Kennedy administration and expanding during the Johnson administration, the U.S. evolved a policy of unconditionally supporting the State of Israel both militarily, economically and diplomatically. This unconditional support has prevented the U.S from being an unbiased broker between the Arab states and Israel, thereby hindering efforts to achieve any level of stability.

The Cold War between the Western democracies and the Soviet Union introduced a whole new set of geopolitical complications for U.S. policy makers. Western efforts to contain Soviet expansionism led to U.S. support for unsavory autocratic regimes such as that of the Shah of Iran, resulting in alienation of ordinary citizens and the rise of anti-American sentiment throughout the Middle East. A number of the autocratic regimes that the U.S. attempted to enlist in opposing the Soviet Union, were also staunchly anti-Israel. The resulting conflicts led to oil embargos and oil supply disruptions, all of which negatively affected the U.S. economy.

Despite efforts over the years to minimize the impact of conflicting goals on broader U.S. policy, the same issues continue to surface today, most notably in the Syrian Civil War, and the related Islamic State crisis. The Syrian Civil War began in the spring of 2011 as a series of protests demanding democratic reforms and the release of political prisoners. At this point, in the interest of preventing a major conflict, it probably would have been possible to enlist Iran and Russia to influence President Bashar al-Assad to accede to some of the demands of the protesters and diffuse the conflict. Instead the U.S. looked at the conflict in geopolitical terms and, seeing an opportunity to weaken Iran and its ally Hezbollah, demanded that "Assad must go." Iran and Hezbollah were never going to allow this to happen and, as Assad responded with increasingly deadly violence, the uprisings evolved into a full-fledged Civil War, a war that has led to a major humanitarian and refugee crisis, destabilizing the whole region.

As ISIS, taking advantage of the regional chaos and instability, has expanded its area of control in Iraq and Syria, the U.S. response, once again, reflects conflicting policy goals. In Iraq U.S. troops are fighting the Islamic State alongside the Shiite-dominated Iraqi government and its ally Iran. In Syria the U.S., in a continuing effort to overthrow the Shiite government of Bashar al-Assad, is supporting and arming the Sunni rebel groups, many of whom are allied with ISIS. Secretary of State John Kerry has attempted to enlist the so-called moderate Sunni Arab states, Turkey, Qatar, and Saudi Arabia, into the anti-ISIS coalition, the same states that have been supporting ISIS against the Assad regime. These policy goals that are at cross-purposes make it very difficult to craft a coherent strategy.

Changing this dynamic, which would demand that the United States make some hard choices, continues to be very difficult. Politicians in democracies are notorious for their inability to make tough decisions, particularly choices among those who all have strong political constituencies. The current situation is no different. The most likely outcome is that we will continue to muddle through, hope for the best and resolve nothing.

CHAPTER 8
Declining Influence

Recent polling of the American people has shown that Americans increasingly believe that the U.S. no longer has the need and or the ability to intervene in the affairs of other nations. In a Pew Center for the People and the Press: America's Place in the World poll taken in 2013 showed that 53 percent of Americans believed the U.S. to be *less* important and powerful than 10 years ago. Holding the contrary view were another 17 percent who thought the U.S. was *more* important and powerful than 10 years ago—a 40-year low. The Pew report said, "The public thinks that the nation does too much to solve world problems, and increasing percentages want the U.S. to 'mind its own business internationally' and pay more attention to problems here at home." "There is strong public sentiment against the United States intervening in the fighting in Syria between government forces and anti-government groups. Nearly two-thirds (64 percent) say the United States does not have a responsibility to do something about the conflict in Syria. Similar percentages oppose the U.S. and its allies bombing Syrian military forces to protect anti-government groups, as they did in Libya, and sending arms and military supplies to those fighting the government of President Bashar al-Assad.[23]

Fear, however, is a powerful motivating factor. As ISIS began to assert itself in Syria and Iraq in 2014, conquering broad tracts of territory, initiating a campaign of terror including suicide bombings, public beheadings and crucifixions, publicizing their brutality on social media, public opinion began to shift in favor of a more activist U.S. approach to the Middle East. By January 2015 a Brookings Institution poll showed that 70 percent of Americans viewed ISIS as the number one threat to American interests and 41 percent supported sending ground troops into Syria to confront ISIS.[24] By the end of 2015, a CNN/*USA Today*/Gallup poll showed that 45 percent felt that the U.S. should take the leading role in solving international problems and 53 percent favored sending ground troops to Iraq or Syria.[25]

The Obama administration, having campaigned on a platform of ending America's Middle East involvement, inherently predisposed to caution when it came to military intervention, wary of a repetition of the financial black holes that the wars in Iraq and Afghanistan created, was reluctant to make a major military commitment to the battle against ISIS. However, faced with the political realities, upcoming elections and criticism by political opposition and media pundits, the Obama administration felt the need to "do something."

Since so much of America's influence in the Middle East has relied on military power and coercive diplomacy, it was difficult for the U.S. to influence events and to protect American interests without deploying the military. Neither allies such as Israel, Saudi Arabia and Turkey nor adversaries such as Iran, Syria and Hezbollah have been willing to follow America's lead and join a coalition to confront ISIS.

How We Got Here:

Soft Power Wins for Iran (Blog from 10/20/2010)

Critics of the George W. Bush administration have frequently cited his reliance on "hard power," particularly military force, to achieve U.S. foreign policy objectives as a major cause of declining U.S. popularity and effectiveness around the world. Although she generally agreed with Bush administration policies, particularly in the Middle East, Hillary Clinton attempted to differentiate herself from the Bush administration policies and Barack Obama's emphasis on "soft power" during the run up to the 2008 election by coining the phrase "smart power."

As we have discovered by observing Secretary of State Clinton in action, her definition of "smart power' is significantly different from "soft power." For her, "smart power" is an attempt to put a softer face on "hard power." As she is discovering, it is very hard to put a soft face on drone attacks, "crippling sanctions" and ongoing occupations.

"Soft Power," on the other hand, consists of persuading others to do what you want because they see convergence between your interests and their interests. They understand your respect for their interests and appreciate your assistance in achieving them. We can better see the effective use of "soft power" by observing Iranian President Mahmoud Ahmadinejad's recent visit to Lebanon.

During the visit Ahmadinejad met with Christian President Suleiman, Sunni Prime Minister Hariri as well as Shia leaders of Hezbollah. He toured the country in an open vehicle welcomed by adoring crowds. Western media and leaders have tried to portray the visit as "provocation" and an attempt to subvert the "pro-western" government of Saud Hariri. Alastair Crooke, a former British Intelligence officer and Director of the Beirut based *Conflicts Forum*, paints a different picture in a recent post:

> Iran's popularity on the streets should not surprise anyone. It is real, and it is heartfelt—and extends beyond the Shia in the south of Beirut. Having been present here in Beirut throughout the war of 2006, I experienced the almost universal shock at how leaders and so-called 'friends of Lebanon' such as Tony Blair and Condoleezza Rice tried to fend-off and delay a ceasefire—in order to allow Israel more time to 'finish the job,' (i.e., to destroy more bridges, more infrastructure and impose civilian casualties) as our 'price' to be paid for Hezbollah's seizure of Israeli soldiers. Feelings here are still raw on this point, and all sectors of opinion know that the only real support for Lebanon in those dark hours came from Syria and Iran. Unsurprisingly, there was a direct element of gratitude in expression to Iran in recent days both for the support then, and its subsequent economic assistance to repair the damage.[26]

The clear winners in the Iraq war have been Iran and the larger Shia community. By finding common interests with potential allies and working with these allies to achieve their common interests, Iran has effectively exploited this victory and increased its regional influence. The hard liners in Tehran also have been able to exploit U.S.-led sanctions, which are making life difficult for ordinary Iranians, to improve their internal position. Soft power works.

A Foreign Policy Success? (Blog from 1/18/2011)

As the referendum on the separation of South Sudan from the north appears to be reaching a relatively peaceful conclusion after years of unrest and civil war, we may be witnessing a rare U.S. foreign policy success. The conflict between the central government of Sudan and the tribal regions in the south and west is long standing and dates to British colonial rule. The British colonial authorities concentrated power in Khartoum and disadvantaged the outlying areas. This pattern continued after independence.

Shortly after taking office in 2009, President Obama appointed, with much fanfare, a number of "special envoys" with responsibility for managing specific foreign policy issues. These included the late Richard Holbrooke in Afghanistan and Pakistan, George Mitchell in Israel/Palestine and Dennis Ross in Iran. Without much fanfare he also appointed General J. Scott Gration as special envoy to Sudan.

At the time, some of us asked the question, "What circumstances and qualities need to be in place for a special envoy to be successful?" I concluded that in order to have any possibility of success there needs to be the right situation, the right envoy and support at the top. None of these were in place for Holbrooke, Mitchell and Ross. However, in the case of General Gration, we had a low-key envoy who was willing to work with all parties to find a solution. The situation in Sudan was relatively isolated from outside influences and General Gration appears to have had the support of both Secretary of State Clinton and President Obama.

As Gration and his fellow diplomats assigned to this issue, Assistant Secretary of State for African Affairs, Johnnie Carson, and special envoy Princeton Lyman, worked to forge compromises among the Sudanese and to persuade the influential Chinese that it was in their interest to have a peaceful and stable outcome, Clinton and Obama had his back. This allowed him to fend off attacks by UN Ambassador Susan Rice and the Save Darfur activists who seemed to want to blow up the whole deal by attacking Sudan.

While there seems to be good will emerging on all sides, a peaceful outcome is clearly not a done deal. The Abyei border region between north and south is a volatile mixture of oil, long-standing tribal animosities and nomadic versus settled lifestyle. Finding a peaceful, workable solution in an area where everybody has a weapon will be a difficult task. If Gration and his team can accomplish this, I would nominate them for the Nobel Prize, because they will have actually accomplished something for the cause of peace.

America's Declining Influence (Blog from 11/1/2011)

This week Palestine was admitted as a full member of UNESCO, the UN Educational, Scientific and Cultural Organization. Despite strong U.S. and Israeli lobbying against the resolution, the vote in favor was overwhelmingly positive: 107 for, 14 against and 52 abstentions. It appears that, besides the U.S. and Israel, only 12 states support the Zionist enterprise. The result was enormously popular among conference members and was enthusiastically received despite the potential financial problems that will be created for the organization. The larger implication is for U.S. global influence.

Immediately after the UNESCO result was determined, the U.S. announced it planned to withhold its $80 million contribution payment to UNESCO, which amounts to 22 percent of the agency's budget. Should the U.S. continue in arrears for two years, it will lose its voting membership and join such luminaries as Somalia and Libya in being in arrears on its UNESCO dues. While the funding deficit is serious, it could easily be made up by countries such as Russia, China or Saudi Arabia who voted yes and for whom $80 million is pocket change. A similar outcome can be expected if Palestine continues to take its statehood case to other UN agencies such as IAEA (International Atomic Energy Agency), WHO (World Health Organization) and 12 other agencies who have similar rules. This will have important implications for U.S. national interest in issues such as Iran's nuclear program and global health among others.

This is only the latest in a series of events, which have highlighted the America's declining influence in the Middle East. When the U.S. demanded that Israel halt construction of settlements in occupied

Palestine, Israeli Prime Minister Netanyahu was completely comfortable in ignoring the wishes of his strongest ally and continuing construction. Likewise, despite U.S. threats to cut off funding to the Palestinian Authority and to veto the statehood resolution at the UN, President Abbas ignored the U.S. threats and proceeded to the UN Security Council.

The decline in U.S. influence in the region and the concurrent rise in Iranian influence began with the U.S. invasion of Iraq. This has had significant consequences for U.S. regional policy. In Iraq, Iran's political allies have been able to prevent the U.S. from retaining a significant military force on the ground. In Bahrain, the U.S. has had to back away from its support of the democracy movements for fear of Iranian influence among Bahrain's Shia majority. When I recently asked a senior State Department official about this, his reply was, "This is an extremely difficult problem."

Absent a significant change in policy approach, it is likely that America's influence with friend and foe alike will continue to decline. The decline will have major implications for America's foreign policy objectives. Other countries will certainly fill the vacuum. Whether this will be positive or negative remains to be seen.

That said, consider Ambassador Charles Freeman's words at the recent NCUSAR (National Council on U.S. Arab Relations) Conference: "I want to close by affirming my faith in the adaptability and resilience of the United States. With all the problems we have made for ourselves and our friends in the Middle East, we have just about run out of alternatives to doing the right things. Now we may get around to actually doing them."

After the Election: What Now? (Blog from 11/9/2012)

After months of campaign wrangling, the presidential election is now behind us and we are left with the question: What will U.S. Middle East policy look like going forward? Since the election campaign was largely devoid of any discussion or debate on policy options, pundits are left to speculate based on a combination of hope, realities and educated guesses. Some things are clear. The major winner from the election outcome was Nate Silver, *The New York Times* statistics blogger, who got the results exactly right. (He said the race would be close, but never in doubt.) The major loser was Israeli Prime Minister Benjamin Netanyahu, who bet big time on the wrong horse. On everything else we can only speculate and wait and see what will happen. In general, not much is likely to change.

The Syrian civil war drags on with the death toll on all sides rising with each passing day. Obama has little choice but to support the rebels rhetorically and with some modest aid, while relying on the wealthy Gulf States to do the heavy lifting of arming the rebels. Americans are in no mood to get entangled in another Middle East ground conflict. Iran and its allies will continue to support the Assad regime. Any negotiated settlement would require engagement with Iran. This would acknowledge Iran's role as a regional player and is an anathema to Washington's foreign policy wizards. The biggest losers will be the Syrian people.

The so-called "Arab Awakening" will likely continue on its own path with the U.S. having little influence on the outcomes. The road to functioning democracies in Egypt, Tunisia and Libya will be bumpy with an ending that is not likely to be friendly to U.S. ambitions for regional control. There is little the U.S. can do to influence the ending except to continue to support them and hope for the best. Hopefully, Congress will not mess it up.

As the "Arab Awakening" spreads to authoritarian U.S. allies in the Gulf region and Jordan, the U.S. will face some uncomfortable choices. With U.S. bases in place and the U.S. requiring Arab support for its anti-Iran policies, the policy has been to offer soft encouragement for reform, but no direct regime criticism. As the regimes crack down more aggressively on dissidents, this policy may become more untenable. Again, I expect that the U.S. will continue current policies and hope for the best.

In Israel/Palestine, Prime Minister Netanyahu has lost all credibility with the Obama administration. His antics have left him on the outside looking in. However, I believe that Obama has realized that a "two-state solution" is no longer possible. Given Israeli intransigence and control of Congress, and Palestinian divisions, there is not much that he can do to change the situation. Again, he will continue to be disengaged.

Iran probably offers the best opportunity for improvement. The Iranians have signaled their willingness to compromise by softening their rhetoric, transferring some of their 20 percent enriched uranium to civilian uses and offering to suspend enrichment to higher levels. If the U.S. responds in-kind, the upcoming talks may bear some fruit. The Iranians, however, will not move without some reduction in sanctions. Given that Congress controls the sanctions regime, Obama will have little ability to negotiate in good faith on sanctions. Promising to consider reducing sanctions at some time in the future will not cut it.

All of this "ignoring the problems" and "hoping for the best," reminds me of the Bill Clinton administration when President Clinton told a State Department official that he was not particularly interested in foreign policy issues because none of his voters were interested. The response was "Sometimes, Mr. President, foreign policy issues find you." Usually, at the most inopportune time.

Is There a Syrian Strategy? (6/19/2013)

Last week, after much debate and hand wringing, the Obama administration announced that the U.S. would begin to arm the Syrian rebel forces directly. The announcement was made in such a manner that it obscured more than clarified U.S. policy with respect to this bloody two-year conflict. It remains vague what sort of weapons will be supplied, who will receive them, how they will be supplied and what is the expected outcome of this step. It appears that the announcement is mostly a political move by the administration to counter the barrage of criticism that it has received from friend and foe for failing to be more aggressive in supporting the rebels. The announcement focused exclusively on tactics and did nothing to clarify U.S. strategy.

The Assad regime and its supporters, on the other hand, appear to have a clear strategy. It is evident that Hezbollah and Iran see the collapse of the Assad government and its replacement by an unfriendly government dominated by radical Sunni fundamentalists as an existential threat. Iran relies on Hezbollah to provide a deterrent force to prevent an Israeli attack and Hezbollah relies on a continuing flow of arms from Iran through Syria to enable them to prevent an Israeli attack on Lebanon. They, therefore, appear committed to doing everything possible to prevent the fall of Assad. Iran is providing arms and advisers and Hezbollah is providing leadership and well-trained, effective urban fighters. Their strategy is to recapture critical roads, junctions and population centers in order to prevent the flow of arms and fighters to the rebel armies. In this, they have been quite successful.

In the face of this progress by the Assad forces, it is unclear how the U.S. arms policy can have much effect. The fundamentalist Gulf monarchies, led by Qatar and Saudi Arabia, have been supplying arms and fighters for months with little to show for it. Assad and his allies have succeeded in cutting supply routes from Jordan and Lebanon. The only remaining route is through Turkey but Turkey is facing its own political upheaval. The Turkish government's support for the rebels is increasingly unpopular as the fighting spills over into Turkish territory. The rebel's efforts have been reduced to conducting terrorist attacks in Syrian cities.

If this modest step by Obama has little or no effect, the pressure will increase to "do more." If the strategy is to overthrow Assad, success will require increasing military intervention, which will risk entering a quagmire or a potential confrontation with Iran, Hezbollah and possibly Russia. If the strategy is to bleed Iran and Hezbollah until they are too weak to resist U.S./Israel, we need to be prepared for more stories of bloodshed and refugees over a long period of time. If we are looking for a negotiated settlement, we will need to include Iran in the negotiations and be prepared for a settlement that leaves in power a government acceptable to Iran. Whatever the strategy, the American people deserve to know what it is and the consequences of that choice.

The Death of Sykes-Picot (Blog from 8/24/2013)

During WWI (the "war to end all wars") British Diplomat Sir Mark Sykes and his French counterpart François Georges-Picot negotiated the now infamous Sykes-Picot Agreement, which was intended to divide up the remnants of the Ottoman Empire into British and French spheres of influence. The resulting hodgepodge of artificial entities controlled by London and Paris was a recipe for conflict from the start. The borders and installed governments largely ignored tribal, ethnic, sectarian and geographic realities in establishing the entities. As David Fromkin points out in his seminal book "A Peace to End All Peace," "It (the agreement) showed that Sir Mark Sykes and his colleagues had adopted policies for the Middle East without first considering whether, in existing conditions, they could feasibly be implemented...and suggested the extent to which the British government did not know what it was getting into when it decided to supersede the Ottoman Empire in Asia..." Now, after almost 100 years of ongoing turmoil, we are witnessing the violent collapse of the ill-conceived political structure in the region.

Of the entities that remained after Sykes-Picot, only Egypt and Iran had any semblance of the characteristics of a nation-state. While Iran is home to numerous ethnic groups, it is united by its overwhelming Shia Muslim character. As the recent Iranian election of Hassan Rouhani with high voter turnout demonstrates, Iran's system of integrating Islamic governance and participatory politics continues to have the support of most Iranians living in the country. Iran is emerging as a more confident and cohesive state. Egypt on the other hand is falling apart before our eyes.

The overthrow of the democratically elected Muslim Brotherhood led government by the Egyptian military and its co-conspirators in the Egyptian deep state seems to herald the end of the brief Egyptian experiment with democracy. As a result, the Muslim Brotherhood's mode of coming to power by nonviolently, incrementally invading the centers of governance has been discredited. The al-Qaeda "idea" of creating an atmosphere of strife and civil disorder as a vehicle for allowing local Islamic groups to come to power and form Islamic "emirates" through the collapse of the nation-state has gained more credibility. As western democracies tire of the ongoing strife, the resulting "emirates" will be able to throw off the remnants of western hegemony. Al-Qaeda can now plausibly say "I told you so."

The Syrian civil war is likely to result in the breakup of the Syrian state that will spill over into Lebanon, Iraq and Turkey. The ethnic Kurds whose nation-state aspirations were ignored by Sykes-Picot will probably reassert themselves in Syria, Turkey, Iraq and possibly Iran. The autocratic Gulf Monarchies of Qatar, Kuwait, UAE and Saudi

Arabia and their partner in Jordan are torn between the need to support their Sunni co-religionists among the Syrian rebels, a position which increases the possibility of jihadist blowback among their own dissidents, and their hatred for Shia Iran. They seem to have decided to double down in Syria while repressing dissent at home.

Whatever the final outcome, it seems certain that the Sykes-Picot construct, which never evolved into a social contract between governments and governed, is doomed to collapse. U.S. policy makers have no good options and little influence. Intervention will likely make a bad situation worse. It won't be pretty.

CHAPTER 9
Other Actors Arrive

Over the last decade, several regional actors, including Israel, have begun to challenge American dominance and influence on the Middle Eastern stage.

Israel has long been touted as America's greatest ally. However, the U.S. is discovering that even great allies can be difficult to influence and control. Thanks to America's generous aid package ($3.3 billion per year), Israel is the strongest military power in the Middle East. The American Israel Public Affairs Committee (AIPAC) exerts enormous influence over U.S. Middle East policy, constraining U.S. policy options. As U.S. commitment and influence in the region have declined, Israel has become more independent of American interests.

Saudi Arabia, with its enormous oil wealth, its anti-Shia sectarian worldview, its low self-confidence resulting from internal divisions and its lofty geo-political ambitions, has become an unpredictable player on the Middle East scene. The Saudi government structure, with an elderly king and no clear succession plan because of divisions within the royal family, is unstable and divided over policy options. In order to keep the conservative religious leaders at bay, the royal family has allowed the **Wahhabi** clerics to have disproportionate influence over government policies, both foreign and domestic. The Sunni monarchy also has had to wrestle with a restive Shia minority within its own borders and

Wahhabism is an ultraconservative, fundamentalist, puritanical religious movement of Sunni Islam that arose in Saudi Arabia. Funded by the Saudi royal family, its influence has grown in Muslim communities around the world.

123

also just across the causeway in Bahrain. All this said, the massive Saudi oil revenues give Saudi leaders a high level of flexibility in their policy decisions. If the U.S. default position is military force or coercive diplomacy, the Saudi default position, as well as that of the other members of the Gulf Cooperation Council (GCC), is to throw money at the problem.

Iran, despite 35 years of sanctions by the U.S. as well as on and off, hot and cold, wars with the U.S., has remained a major adversary and competitor for influence. With its large, well-educated population, its relatively stable Islamic governance system, its influence within the Shia minorities of its neighbors, its large potential petroleum supplies and its geopolitical size and location, Iran is well-positioned to exert influence and frustrate American policy objectives.

As U.S. influence and willingness to intervene and provide a force for stability has declined, a power vacuum is developing in the Middle East region. This trend has been exacerbated by events of the Arab Awakening that have brought political unrest to a number of American allies and other potential regional actors. The unrest has forced these regional actors to pay more attention to domestic issues rather than projecting influence around the region. Among the non-state actors vying for influence, Hezbollah, the Lebanese social, political and military organization, is the major player. Hamas, an offshoot of the Egyptian Muslim Brotherhood, has governed the Palestinian enclave of Gaza since 2007. However, with the overthrow of the Muslim Brotherhood-led Egyptian government by a military coup d'état in July 2013 and the subsequent re-imposition of the Israeli blockade of Gaza, Hamas' influence has been limited. Al-Qaeda continues to be a factor in Iraq, Yemen, North Africa and, most recently, in Syria as the major force in the Islamic resistance. Its major influence has been to sow chaos at a time when the U.S. is struggling to create some degree of stability.

Although designated as a terrorist group by the U.S. in 1997, Hezbollah essentially functions as a state within a state in Lebanon. It delivers services and operates its military much more effectively than the official Lebanese government. As one Lebanese resident told me, "If you need water or electricity, don't call the government, call Hezbollah." Without Hezbollah, Lebanon would most likely either collapse or be overrun by the Israelis. Hezbollah maintains its own foreign ministry and has good relations with many countries, including some in Europe. Supported by Iran, Hezbollah's militias have been a major factor in propping up the government of **Bashar al-Assad** in Syria. Hezbollah's long-time leader, Hassan Nasrallah, has long been one of the most popular leaders in the Arab world.

Bashar al-Assad is the President of Syria, General Secretary of the Ba'ath Party and Regional Secretary of the party's branch in Syria. He has served as President since 2000, when he succeeded his father, Hafez al-Assad, who led Syria for 30 years until his death.

In 2014, the Islamic State in Iraq and al-Shams (ISIS), born out of the chaos and regional upheaval of the Iraq War and the Syrian Civil War, asserted itself as the major resistance force against U.S. power in the Middle East. Conquering large portions of Iraq and Syria, eliminating the post WWI colonial borders, declaring an Islamic caliphate and inspiring followers around the Middle East and North Africa, ISIS, in a short period of time, has become a force to be reckoned with.

Relations between nation states have long been framed by treaties, multinational organizations and international law. Relations with these non-state powers have been more difficult to manage. For the most part the U.S. has refused to maintain any diplomatic contact with the non-state groups and thus economic coercion and military action have been the only tools in the toolbox. When these tools are not effective, the U.S. is at a loss for a means to have any influence.

Israel Pushes Back

National Self-determination (Blog from 2/21/2008)

Since World War I the U.S., as articulated by President Woodrow Wilson, has tried to balance the concept of national self-determination with the realpolitik need to maintain the nation state system. The tension between the right of a state to maintain its territorial integrity and the right of people to self-determination has caused numerous diplomatic policy headaches. For most of recent history, the U.S. has come down on the side of the stability of nation states, particularly when the states have been sympathetic to U.S. foreign policy goals. With its rapid recognition of the new state of Kosovo following a unilateral declaration of independence by the Kosovars, the U.S. has moved in the other direction. One can make the case that this was the right decision given that an independent Kosovo was probably inevitable following the U.S./NATO intervention in a Serbian civil war in the 1990s. The U.S. claims that this is a "special case" and does not create any precedents. Frank Wisner, U.S. Special Envoy to Kosovo, argues, "Kosovo is a unique case." Not everybody agrees. Russia has refused to recognize an independent Kosovo, supporting its Slavic brothers in Serbia. Spain and Greece also have said that they will not recognize and independent Kosovo fearing an empowering precedent for their restive Basque and Turkmen minorities. Israel also is trying to decide how it will deal with the problem. Statements by some Palestinian Authority ministers suggesting that the PLO also should unilaterally declare independence and pressure the international community for recognition have caused consternation on the part of those who hope for a negotiated two-state solution. Others in Palestine and the international community have begun to be more vocal in advocating disbanding the PLO altogether, turning the whole problem over to the Israelis and pressing for one man, one vote. Israeli Prime Minister Ehud Olmert labeled this "the South African solution." This is the worst-case scenario for Israelis, as demographics would mean the end of the "Jewish State." For this to happen, Palestinian politicians would need to give up their power voluntarily; not something politicians do easily. However, as the post Annapolis negotiations continue to drag on with no signs of progress, an "out of the box" solution becomes more and more likely.

Israel Ignores the U.S. (Blog from 7/16/2008)

This week Israel and Hezbollah completed a prisoner exchange agreement mediated by Germany under which five Lebanese Hezbollah fighters and 200 bodies of deceased fighters, Lebanese and Palestinian, were exchanged for the bodies of the two Israel Defense Force (IDF) soldiers who were kidnapped by Hezbollah in 2006.

Israel also has been negotiating with Hamas using Egypt as the intermediary. Thus far, the outcome has been a ceasefire in Gaza, which has (for the most part) held, and it appears that a prisoner exchange will occur, followed by a gradual opening of the Gaza border crossings and easing of the blockade that has starved the Gaza economy.

All this, plus ongoing peace negotiations with Syria, mediated by U.S. ally Turkey, has taken place despite fierce opposition from Martin Indyk, the U.S.'s former ambassador to Israel and currently Director of The Washington Institute for Near East Policy, a pro Israel think tank, who said in a lecture in Ketchum, Idaho that the U.S. said to Israel "don't you dare talk to Hezbollah, Hamas and Syria."

The fact that Israel ignores the U.S. is not particularly surprising. Israeli war hero and Chief of Staff of the IDF, Moshe Dayan, once said, "The U.S. gives us money, guns and advice. We choose to take their money and guns and ignore their advice." Ambassador Indyk said that negotiating with these three adversaries makes sense for Israel. The purpose is to co-opt these Iranian allies so that Israel will be free to attack Iran without fear of retaliation from its close neighbors.

This may work for Israel, but how does it work for their erstwhile Palestinian negotiating partner Mahmoud Abbas (also known as Abu Mazen)? Following last year's Annapolis conference, U.S./Israel policy was to isolate Hezbollah, Hamas and Syria and strengthen Abu Mazen and Fatah with money, arms and political backing. In return, Fatah would negotiate with Israel toward a peace framework. After months of fruitless negotiations, Fatah has accomplished almost nothing to benefit the Palestinian people, and Israel has refused to release prisoners, stop settlement building or remove checkpoints and has continued attacks on the West Bank.

Hezbollah and Hamas, whose approach is confrontation, resistance and occasional violence, have been successful. Hezbollah was even clever enough to demand the release of Palestinians in the prisoner exchange. They now can say to the Palestinian people, "See. We told you that negotiating with Israel is futile. The only thing that they respond to is force." With Palestinian elections probably upcoming, Fatah is in a weaker position with respect to Hamas than they were last week and U.S. policy is in shambles.

Is Anything Happening? (Blog from 4/22/2009)

U.S. Middle East envoy George Mitchell was back in the region last week. After a high-profile kickoff to Middle East diplomacy featuring visits to the region by Mitchell and Secretary of State Hillary Clinton, things have been pretty quiet on the Washington front.

Given the priority of dealing with the economic crisis and Senator Mitchell's preference for quiet diplomacy, this is not at all surprising. I have never been a big fan of diplomacy by pronouncement and press conference that was the hallmark of the Bush administration. Soon the Obama administration will need to make clear the policies that it will put forward to deal with the Palestine question, which is the cornerstone for progress on all other issues in the region.

When I was last in the region in November, there were great expectations that a more balanced U.S. policy would lead to progress in reaching a peace agreement. Regional leaders understood that Obama had bigger priorities to deal with, such as Iraq, Afghanistan and the economy, which would occupy his attention. However, this window of opportunity will not remain open forever.

Likud is the major center-right party in Israel and was founded in 1973 by Menachem Begin in an alliance with several right-wing and liberal parties.

There certainly is a lot of disagreement within the administration about what sort of policy should emerge. On one side you have Dennis Ross (an incrementalist and "Israel's lawyer"), Rahm Emmanuel ("Our man in the White House" according to his Zionist father), and Vice President Joe (I am a Zionist) Biden and on the other side George Mitchell (meticulously even-handed) and National Security Adviser James Jones.

Benjamin Netanyahu is the current prime minister of Israel.

Among the thorny issues are how to deal with the right wing Israeli government of **Likud** Party leader **Benjamin Netanyahu** and what sort of relationship to have with Hamas. Despite encouragement by outside experts and former diplomats to engage with Hamas, thus far the Obama administration has continued the Bush policy of refusing to deal with

Hamas unless it recognizes Israel as a Jewish state, endorses previous agreements and renounces violence. This policy has always been a non-starter.

Many Israelis are concerned about a confrontation between Netanyahu and the Obama administration over efforts to establish a Palestinian state. The Israeli newspaper Haaretz wrote:

> In an unprecedented move, the Obama administration is readying for a possible confrontation with Prime Minister Benjamin Netanyahu by briefing Democratic congressmen on the peace process and the positions of the new government in Israel regarding a two-state solution.
>
> The Obama administration is expecting a clash with Netanyahu over his refusal to support the establishment of a Palestinian state alongside Israel.[27]

Waiting for the Messiah (Blog from 10/14/2013)

Since Secretary of State John Kerry kicked off the latest round of negotiations between Israel and the Palestinian Authority designed to reach a two-state solution to the Israel/Palestine situation, we have heard next to nothing about what is happening. This could be either good news or bad news. It is possible (although unlikely) that progress is being made behind the scene in substantive negotiations that are best done out of the media spotlight. A more likely scenario is that nothing is happening and all sides are concerned about the potential for unrest that would accompany the final demise of the two-state solution.

Politicians on all sides have been declaring that "the window for a two-state solution will close within a year" for the last 15 years. This dire prediction has become as common as Israel's 20-year prediction that, absent a military attack, Iran will have a nuclear weapon within six months. While an Iranian nuclear weapon would constitute a serious threat to Israel, the Reut Institute, an Israeli think tank that advises Israeli leaders on strategic issues, has concluded that the biggest threat to Israeli national security is "one man, one vote." In a recent report Reut stated, "Annexation of the Palestinian people into Israel would compromise Israel's Jewish majority, while continued control of the Palestinian population may jeopardize Israel's democracy and long-term legitimacy." Most Israelis have resisted this warning since they find the status quo of occupation and separation to be completely sustainable.

Seven years ago, when I first wrote about a single-state solution, I felt the need to label my posts: "A Completely Absurd Idea." Today the one bi-national state can now be discussed in polite company. Many young people in Palestine have completely gone to one state-ism. At a Sabeel conference last week, I heard a Palestinian leader describe his conversations with his young daughters. One daughter is a second-year chemical engineering major at M.I.T. and the other is a sophomore at the Ramallah Friends School. They said, "Dad, 1948 was like a hundred 9/11s and you and grandpa reacted like anyone would. First you tried fighting (we're not very good fighters), then you tried non-violent resistance, then you tried negotiating and then you tried going to the UN. Dad, nothing worked. We are still occupied. Why don't we just say to the Israelis, okay you win. You get it all. The land, the water, the oil and gas in Gaza and, by the way, you also get us. I understand that you have free healthcare. Where do I pick up my card? I would also like your free education. And where do I go to vote?"

The reality is that we already have a single state. The only question is, what kind of a state it will be. Will it be an apartheid state under occupation, an ethnically cleansed Jewish state or a bi-national state with equal rights for all? Waiting for two states is like the Jewish view of waiting for the Messiah. He may come someday, but I am not holding my breath.

Shifting Sands in the Middle East

The Landscape Changes Again (Blog from 9/20/2013)

The rise of the Arab Awakening, which began with so much promise before its subsequent decent into chaos, has drastically changed the geopolitical landscape in the Middle East and North Africa. Libya and Tunisia are mired in political turmoil. Egypt is teetering on the brink of civil conflict. Syria is deeply engaged in a full-scale civil war with no end in sight. Yemen's civil unrest is not yet a civil war, but with its separationist history, civil conflict is certainly possible. Iraq is experiencing as much sectarian violence as during the dark days of the "surge." Lebanon is threatened by collapse as outside forces play out their geopolitical goals. Only Hezbollah's balancing efforts and refusal to play the sectarian card are keeping Lebanon stable. Jordan is trying desperately to avoid spillover from its unstable neighbors.

In all these countries that experienced transition from decades-long authoritarian rule to some form of democracy, neither the leaders nor the international community realized that the people didn't necessarily want democracy. What they wanted was a better life and to be treated better by their government. None of the leaders, who succeeded the authoritarian rulers, whether they were Islamist or secular, had any vision about how to move their countries ahead.

The result of all this is that the region has become a playground for jihadists who hold an al-Qaeda like worldview. Trained in Saudi Arabia's Wahhabi tradition, they have arrived from around the world, including Europe and the U.S., in order to fight for their vision of an Islamic caliphate. While the bulk of the Arab world does not want to be ruled by jihadists and other hardline Islamists, the hardliners are slowly gaining the upper hand. Their success in the region as well as the threat that they pose when they bring their worldview and fighting skills back to their countries of origin, makes these Sunni jihadists the biggest national security threat to the U.S. and other western countries.

This threat has drastically changed the geopolitical calculus in the region. The biggest threat to Israel is no longer an attack by its Arab neighbors, who have bigger problems of their own and have largely lost interest in the Palestinian issue. The Palestinian issue is now an internal Israeli problem. Having established its rule over all of historical Palestine, Israel now has the problem of how to deal with a minority population ruling over the majority, in many cases brutally. History has shown that this is not a recipe for stability.

As the Sunni jihadists have become the major security threat, Saudi Arabia's support and funding of these characters has made Saudi Arabia part of the problem and not part of the solution. Can the U.S.

maintain its close relationship with Saudi Arabia while trying to deal with the mounting jihadist threat?

The Sunni jihadist threat also has implications for U.S. and western relations with Iran. Iran, a predominately Shia country, has the same concerns about the Sunni jihadists as do the western countries. This makes Iran a natural ally in combating this threat. Combine this fact with the charm offensive initiated by Iranian President Hassan Rouhani and we may have an opening for rapprochement between Iran and the west. Israel and Saudi Arabia would not be happy, but occasionally western countries have acted in their own national interest. Openings have been there before and have been rebuffed. This time may be different.

Iran Looks for Influence and Respect

EU+3/Iran Nuclear Agreement: On November 24, 2013 in Geneva, EU High Representative Catherine Ashton, together with the Foreign Ministers of China, France, Germany, Russia, the United Kingdom and the United States, successfully concluded a meeting at which an agreement (known as the Joint Plan of Action) was reached with Iran on a first step toward a comprehensive and verifiable diplomatic solution to concerns about the Iranian nuclear program.

Obstacles to an Agreement with Iran
(Blog from 12/9/2013)

Before digging into the political dynamics surrounding the recently signed **EU+3/Iran nuclear agreement**, it is important to understand some of the history. The U.S. sanctions regimen against Iran began in 1979 shortly after the Iranian Revolution and the subsequent U.S. embassy hostage crisis. The initial sanctions were imposed by President Jimmy Carter who froze millions of dollars of Iranian assets in U.S. banks. In the 1980s, as the U.S. attempted to aid Saddam Hussein during the Iran-Iraq war, the sanctions were expanded to include weapons and financial aid to Iran. The sanctions regime was expanded in 1987 under

President Ronald Reagan and again in 1997 under President Bill Clinton. President Obama has magnified the impact of the sanctions by threatening and coercing governments around the world, wishing to do business in the U.S., to abide by the unilateral American sanctions. These sanctions have had an increasingly negative impact on the Iranian economy and on the lives of ordinary Iranians. Circumventing and mitigating the effects of the sanctions has been a major focus of almost all Iranian governments.

The Iranian nuclear program dates back to 1957 when the U.S. signed a nuclear cooperation agreement with Mohammad Reza Shah Pahlavi's government under the Atoms for Peace program. Following the revolution, the Siemens AG contract to build the Bushehr nuclear reactor was terminated. Shortly thereafter the Iranian government announced an ambitious program to construct its own reactor and to master the nuclear fuel cycle. In my opinion, while the nuclear program has been expanded to provide nuclear power and medical isotopes, its primary purpose has been to accumulate bargaining chips in order get the sanctions removed or reduced and to get Iran reintegrated into the international community. As the West has rebuffed all Iranian efforts at reintegration, the chips have continued to accumulate. It is not a nuclear weapon that concerns the U.S. and its allies, Israel and Saudi Arabia, but the reintegration of Iran into the global economy.

Iran is strategically located astride the Strait of Hormuz and is a buffer state between the Middle East and Central Asia. With its large (70mm), well-educated, young population, relatively stable governance, and substantial potential for oil and gas production, Iran is much better positioned than its neighbors to project political and economic power, both within the region and globally. It is this potential to change the status quo in the region that most worries Iran's adversaries. The nuclear weapons issue is a politically powerful red herring to cover the true concerns.

During the Geneva talks, Israel and Saudi Arabia spent much money, printers' ink and bombast to prevent the interim agreement from being signed. Having failed in that effort, they are now rolling out the political big guns in Washington in order shoot down any final comprehensive deal that will result in rapprochement with Iran. Already the Obama administration is showing signs of backing away from any final status agreement. While it is in America's interest to resolve the conflict with Iran diplomatically, it is unclear to me whether or not Obama, who sees every foreign policy issue through a lens of domestic politics, will be able to summon the political will to deliver on the promise of the Geneva agreement.

Hamas Retains its Influence

With Friends Like This, Who Needs Enemies?
(Blog from 1/25/2008)

With the destruction of the border fence between Gaza and Egypt in Rafah and subsequent free flow of traffic back and forth across the border, Hamas has again succeeded in throwing a monkey wrench into the U.S. and Israeli plans to impose their will in this part of the world. Hamas, founded in the 1980s with the assistance of the U.S. and Israel as a counterbalance to the PLO, has long been a problem for the U.S. and Israel and some of their allies in the region. As my friend Palestinian Archbishop Elias Chacour once said to me, "Once the baby is born and grows up, it is hard to control it." Because Hamas is an offshoot of the Egyptian Muslim Brotherhood, the largest opposition political organization in Egypt, the authoritarian Egyptian regime is leery of anything that might increase its strength. Jordan is concerned that any success by Hamas with its Islamist agenda will empower the Islamists within Jordan. For Fatah and the PLO, Hamas is their biggest political rival. Now that Hamas controls Gaza, former senior ministers in the Jordanian government tell me that Jordanian Intelligence believes that Hamas is stronger in the West Bank than Fatah. Ever since Hamas won the general election in 2006, the U.S., Israel and their western allies have portrayed themselves as friends and supporters of Fatah, primarily with guns and money. Worry on Hamas' part that this aid would allow Fatah to destroy them militarily led to the Hamas takeover of Gaza.

One of the first things that Hamas accomplished in Gaza was to disarm all of the factions and criminal gangs in Gaza and make the security forces the only ones with guns. This was a very popular move with average citizens. As one Gazan woman said, "We may not have much money, but at least we can go shopping and visit our friends and family without risking getting killed." Seeing the popularity of this move, Fatah tried to do the same thing in Nablus when Israel turned security there over to them. Israel, however, made it backfire by invading Nablus and arresting many of the people that had just been disarmed. Palestinian Authority President Mahmoud Abbas' strategy has been to show that he can accomplish more to relieve the suffering of the Palestinian people by engaging and compromising with his friends—the U.S. and Israel—than Hamas can accomplish by resistance and confrontation. The problem is that Abbas didn't pick very reliable friends. When Israel completely blockaded Gaza, creating a humanitarian crisis, Abbas, Egypt and Jordan pleaded with the U.S. to do something to help. Nothing happened. Hamas took action by blowing up the border fence. This not only broke the blockade, but created diplomatic chaos in Israel, Egypt and the U.S. They have been issuing conflicting and contradictory statements by the hour. Hamas has asked that the border be reestablished, but that the border be open and controlled. The U.S. has threatened Egypt with the loss of aid if they do so. Israel isn't sure what to say. One thing that is for certain: Hamas will come out of this stronger, and Fatah and its "friends" will be weaker.

Which Prisoners Will Be Released?
(Blog from 2/25/2009)

Shortly after Hamas won a substantial majority in the Palestinian Legislative Council (PLC) 2006 election, Israel arrested over 30 members of the PLC. Those arrested were primarily Hamas representatives and they are still being detained as political prisoners in Israel. Evidently Israel and the U.S. thought that they would be able to deny Hamas a majority in the PLC and that the more compliant Fatah faction would retain control.

The strategy did not quite work out as planned. Hamas promptly boycotted the PLC, preventing a quorum and the PLC has not functioned since. President Mahmoud Abbas (Abu Mazen) responded by appointing a caretaker government led by Salam Fayyad as Prime Minister. Hamas considers this government illegitimate since it has not received the PLC vote of confidence required by the Palestinian Basic Law. Hamas also considers President Abbas an illegitimate President saying that his term expired on January 9, 2009.

Since Israel and Hamas declared unilateral ceasefires ending the Gaza war, there have been ongoing negotiations between Israel and Hamas on a more permanent long-term ceasefire. One of the points of contention has been the release of prisoners. Israel wants the release of captured Israeli soldier Gilad Shalit and Hamas wants over 1,000 Palestinian prisoners to be released by Israel. This prisoner exchange will likely happen at some point. Israel has long been reluctant to release prisoners with "blood on their hands," but since the Hamas PLC members are political prisoners they likely will be among those released.

This event will have a significant impact on the political dynamic in the region. The PLC will be reconstituted and likely will remove Prime Minister Fayyad from office and install a Hamas-led government. They also may begin proceedings to remove Abbas from office. These steps could result in new elections.

Since the Gaza war, Hamas' popularity has increased, and polls indicate that they would win any new election. The U.S. and Israel would then be faced with a Palestinian Authority completely under the control of Hamas. Things in the Middle East don't always work out the way you plan. As Egyptian President Gamal Nasser once said, "The genius of you Americans is that you don't have simple stupid policies. You only have really complicated stupid policies."

A Bad Start to Israel/Palestine Negotiations
(Blog from 9/1/2010)

Those involved in this week's much discussed beginning of direct discussions between Palestinian Authority President Mahmoud Abbas and Israeli Prime Minister Benjamin Netanyahu were rudely introduced to the realities of the region when Palestinian gunmen shot and killed four Israeli settlers outside of the city of Hebron on the West Bank. Hamas, which in recent months has observed a ceasefire, immediately claimed responsibility for the attack.

The U.S. mainstream media has described the attack as an effort by

Hamas to sabotage the upcoming talks, citing their refusal to recognize Israel's "right to exist." While only Hamas knows the reasons for initiating the attack, my take is somewhat different.

Based on my discussions with Hamas leaders, I believe that Hamas would accept a solution that was based on the 1967 borders, East Jerusalem as the capital of the Palestinian state, a just solution for the refugees and approval by the Palestinian people in a referendum. On May 5, 2009, **Khaled Mashal** said similar things to *The New York Times*, "Hamas has accepted the national reconciliation document. It has accepted a Palestinian state on the 1967 borders including East Jerusalem, dismantling settlements, and the right of return based on a long-term truce."[28]

> **Khaled Mashal** is the Political Director of the Palestinian political organization Hamas.

So why initiate the attack at this time? If the reason was to sabotage the negotiations, the attack was completely unnecessary. The talks will most likely fail without any help from Hamas.

I think that Hamas is trying to send two messages. One is that Hamas cannot be ignored in any negotiations. They are a player and, as indicated by their victory in the 2006 elections, they speak for a large number of Palestinians. The U.S., Israel and the Palestinian Authority ignore them at their own peril.

The second message is that the status quo is not sustainable. For the past two decades since the Oslo Accords, Israel's policy toward the "peace process" has been to have all process and no peace. Through the use of walls, barriers, settlements, attacks, targeted killings and arrests, Israel has succeeded in maintaining the occupation with a modicum of calm. They are perfectly content to have the negotiations either fail, with the Palestinians being blamed, or drag on endlessly. Hamas' message is that it is not going to allow this scenario to be perpetuated indefinitely. It is significant that the deadly attack occurred in an area of the West Bank totally controlled by the Israelis.

It is unlikely that the U.S. will hear this message, and consequently, more innocent civilians will die on both sides.

Gaza: Winners and Losers (Blog from 11/23/2012)

As of today the ceasefire agreement between Hamas and Israel, negotiated by Egyptian President Mohamed Morsi, appears to be holding. (The only violation has been the killing of a Gazan farmer by an Israeli soldier. Hamas' reaction was relatively muted. They seem to want to give peace a chance.) As in any armed conflict, it is difficult to say that anybody won when almost 200 people were killed on both sides. That said, it is possible to point out some winners and losers.

Winners:

Hamas: In any conflict such as this in which the power equation is so unbalanced, the weaker side wins by not losing and the stronger side loses by not winning. Hamas in Gaza was able to absorb over 1,500 airstrikes and live to fight another day. Hamas' popularity, both in Gaza and the West Bank, has soared. Their strategic objectives of ceasing the bombing raids, stopping the targeted killings and easing the blockade of Gaza have been agreed to in the ceasefire agreement. It remains to be seen whether or not Israel will implement the agreement. If not, we may be back in the same mess a few weeks from now. Hamas' political capital in the region also has been enhanced by statements of support and by numerous visits by ranking Arab officials.

Egyptian President Mohamed Morsi: Morsi's key role in brokering the ceasefire agreement has raised his personal status, as well as that of Egypt.

Iran: Iran's game-changing supply of longer range weapons and missile technology to Hamas has helped to cement their relationship. In addition, Iran had a chance to watch the much-vaunted Israeli "Iron Dome" missile defense system in action and to better assess its strengths and weaknesses. In the event of an Iran-Israel conflict, this information will certainly be helpful to the Iranian military.

Losers:

Israeli Prime Minister Benjamin Netanyahu: The last thing that Netanyahu needed, two months before an election, was to have his arm twisted into agreeing to a ceasefire agreement that is enormously unpopular with the Israeli population. A snap poll conducted shortly after the ceasefire was announced showed that 70 percent of the respondents disagreed with the decision to sign the ceasefire agreement and supported a ground war in Gaza.

Palestinian Authority President Mahmoud Abbas: The U.S.-supported Abbas was completely sidelined during the whole process. His already low standing among Palestinians has plummeted.

To be determined:

President Obama and Hillary Clinton: While this is based on speculation on my part, it is hard for me to imagine that Netanyahu would have agreed to this ceasefire without some serious pressure from the U.S. Obama's adroit handling of the relationship with Morsi and Clinton's persuasion of Netanyahu (I would love to know what she said!) may bode well for U.S. relationships in the Middle East.

Hezbollah: A State Within a State

Who Won? (Blog from 8/20/2006)

As the conflict between Israel and Hezbollah has reached a stalemated ceasefire as everyone seems to be claiming victory. George Bush, Ehud Olmert, **Hassan Nasrallah** and Prime Minister Ahmadinejad of Iran have all announced that their side has emerged victorious in the military conflict. It seems to me that there can be no victors in a conflict where over one thousand innocent civilians have perished to reestablish what Condi Rice calls the "status quo ante." You might be able to argue that Hezbollah won because they didn't lose and Israel lost because they didn't win, but that is a pretty pyrrhic victory. It is, however, clear who is winning the political battle. Hezbollah and Iran have emerged as the clear victors on the political front. While the west has dithered and the Lebanese government has talked, Hezbollah, with a blank check from Iran, is moving rapidly and efficiently to compensate people who have lost their homes to the

Hassan Nasrallah is the longtime leader of Hezbollah.

Israeli bombardment with bundles of cash and promises to rebuild their homes. (Perhaps we should hire them to help with the response to our next major hurricane.)

Hezbollah, Iran and the Syrians have established themselves as major players in the post conflict Middle East. Israel's stated objective in the war was to eliminate Hezbollah south of the Litani River, to destroy its arsenal and to prevent the rearming by Syria—mission impossible. Trying to drive Hezbollah out will not succeed as long as Lebanese Shia come back. It is like New York trying to drive Republicans out of Idaho. As soon as the people come back, the Republicans come back. Hezbollah's fighters are primarily reservists who keep their weapons in their closet and under their beds. When they are needed, they pick up their weapons and head out to fight. The long porous border between Syria and Lebanon makes any attempt to prevent rearmament a hopeless cause.

The only way to accomplish the objectives is to talk to Hezbollah, Syria and Iran. Although Israel's peace-oriented left has lost its voice (much as it has in the U.S.), the realists on the Israeli political scene are beginning to examine the concept of negotiations with Syria and Iran. Amir Peretz, the Israeli Defense Minister, has called for negotiations with Syria. (He was immediately attacked by members of his own party.) Israeli Foreign Minister, Tzipi Livni, has appointed a "project manager" for possible negotiations with Syria. There certainly are those in Israel who are clamoring for another war with Lebanon and the current Israeli government will probably be short lived, but one hopes that reason will prevail. Any negotiations with Syria will bring the Golan Heights into play. The Golan Heights is the strategic high ground in the Galilee. It is understandable why Israel would only agree to relinquish it as part of a firm peace agreement with Syria. Not a bad outcome. Peace agreements with Jordan and Israel have remained stable for a number of years. They may not like each other, but they live alongside each other. Condi Rice said that this conflict is "the birth pangs of a new Middle East." It might not be the new Middle East that she envisioned and the birth did not need to be as painful, but she may have been right for the wrong reasons.

The Lebanese Elections Are Not Over
(Blog from 6/10/2009)

When I was in Lebanon last fall, I met with numerous Lebanese political leaders and American diplomats who said the consensus was that the Hezbollah-led March 8 coalition would win a narrow victory in the parliamentary elections and would be asked to form the next government. U.S. officials were doing everything possible to prevent this outcome by funneling copious amounts of aid through the ruling western-oriented March 14 coalition. They were joined in this endeavor by Egypt and Saudi Arabia on behalf of March 14 and by Iran and Syria on behalf of the March 8 coalition.

So much money has been expended by all sides in vote buying, vote renting, air tickets so ex-pats could vote, etc. that the Lebanese economy has continued to move along at a 7 percent growth rate despite the global recession. After several months of campaigning and mudslinging, the Lebanese people finally got to choose and returned control to the March 14 coalition led by Saad Hariri, the son of assassinated former Prime Minister Rafic Hariri. The Obama administration must have breathed a sigh of relief.

The Western media has portrayed the result as a defeat for Hezbollah, Iran and Syria. In reality, it was a defeat for Hezbollah's ally, Christian leader Michel Aoun and his Free Patriotic Movement (FPM) party. Hezbollah only fielded 11 candidates and was counting on Amal, a Shia party, and FPM to give them a working majority. Although the March 8 coalition received 100,000 more popular votes than March 14, the arcane Lebanese system, which allocates 50 percent of the seats to the Christians even though they are only one-third of the population, resulted in March 14 winning a majority.

Hezbollah leader Hassan Nasrallah accepted the results "in a sporting spirit" and called for cooperation among the parties. This will be tested over the next few weeks as March 14 attempts to form a government. Much depends on whether Hariri or current Prime Minister Fouad Siniora heads the government. When the current unity government was negotiated in Qatar last fall, Hezbollah was given one third of the cabinet seats, which gives them veto power on major decisions. Despite the fact that nothing much has changed, Siniora, under U.S.

pressure, has said the March 14 "won" the election and should govern by itself. This is a non-starter for Hezbollah, who believes in consensus government and could precipitate a governmental crisis.

The Hezbollah Conundrum (Blog from 7/31/2013)

Last week, the European Union succumbed to U.S./Israel pressure and designated the so-called "military wing" of the Lebanese political party/social organization/militia, Hezbollah, as a "terrorist organization." The decision made by politicians in Brussels has left the EU professional diplomats and legal experts with a major mess to sort out. The problems were immediately evident. While an EU spokesperson in Brussels was acclaiming the important consequences of this action, the EU Ambassador to Lebanon, Angelina Eichhorst, was meeting with Hezbollah and other Lebanese leaders in Beirut to explain that this action would have no impact on EU relations with Hezbollah or Lebanon. My reaction was, "Have they lost it?"

Among the problems that this ill-considered action creates is *who* exactly is being blacklisted. There is no clearly defined line between the "military wing" of Hezbollah and its political and social activities. This was demonstrated during the 2006 Israeli invasion of Lebanon. Hezbollah members abandoned their positions as dentists, political figures, farmers etc., reclaimed their AK-47s and grenade launchers from their closets or under their beds and joined the fight against the invader. While there is a professional component to the Hezbollah militia, by and large it is the consummate citizen army.

The U.S. gets around this problem by blacklisting all of Hezbollah. During my last visit to Beirut, I was treated to one of the bizarre consequences of this position when a U.S. diplomat responsible for non-military aid to Lebanon told me that she could not meet with the government minister responsible for disseminating this aid because he was a member of Hezbollah. She had to rely on the Swiss to coordinate with the Lebanese government.

Everyone is puzzled about how the EU will distinguish between the "Civil Wing" and the "Military Wing" of Hezbollah. My friend, Franklin Lamb, an American writer and researcher based in Beirut, describes the issues in a recent article:

According to a lawyer at the American Society of International Law (ASIL) in Washington, D.C., the EU decision was a big mistake from an international law standpoint and could be an international lawyer's worst nightmare or a dream come true. Which would depend if the lawyer was representing the EU in trying to unravel the civil-military conundrum or advising thousands of EU member states' businesses and agencies wanting to continue any business with the Lebanese government, UNIFIL, or countless NGOs who regularly interact with Hezbollah. (sic)

"It's a real legal mess!" the ASIL source explained, as he described the legal confusion the EU action caused. "The best thing for EU credibility and international relations right now on this subject would be for the EU to forget what it did and to desist from any implementation whatsoever. And then let the designation be removed after the six month's trial period as provided by EU regulations. Otherwise, their decision will swamp courtrooms and complicate Middle East-European political and economic relations with challenges from all points on the compass with uncertain outcomes, to say the least."[29]

ISIS Changes the Middle East

Two Countries, One War (Blog from 6/17/2014)

Since the surprise success of the militant Islamist group Islamic State in Iraq and Syria (ISIS), sometimes known as Islamic State in the Levant (ISIL) in seizing territory in Iraq, including the major cities of Mosul and Tikrit, there has been much hand wringing, blame gaming, pontificating and suggestions for U.S. reaction by politicians and pundits. The ability of ISIS to achieve these gains so rapidly surprised not only U.S. intelligence agencies, who have few active assets on the ground, but also Iranian intelligence agencies, who know the situation in Iraq better than anyone except the Iraqis themselves. Also surprising was the ease with which 800 ISIS fighters routed a 30,000-man Iraqi security force, a force the U.S. spent so much blood and treasure to recruit, arm and train. As ISIS moves rapidly toward Baghdad, murdering hundreds of Shia Iraqis on its way, U.S. political and military leaders are faced with very difficult choices concerning the appropriate response.

Some politicians and pundits are calling for air strikes in the Sunni region in support of Iraqi Army forces. The same guys who helped create this mess by invading Iraq and overthrowing Saddam Hussein are calling for the U.S. to redeploy troops in Iraq in order to prevent Iran from increasing its influence with the Iraqi government. Others say that we have no national interest in this situation and should not get involved, letting the regional powers sort it out. In my view, the U.S., looking at the Syrian civil war as a way of weakening Iran and Hezbollah, having supported the insurgent forces in Syria, including ISIS, against the regime of Bashar al-Assad, having encouraged its Persian Gulf allies, such as Saudi Arabia and Qatar, to support the Islamic groups in Syria, having helped to establish an arms trafficking path through Turkey into Syria, has helped to create this problem. It, therefore, has a strong national interest in helping to resolve it. Any outcome that leaves an Islamist group, committed to killing all infidels, deemed too radical to support by al-Qaeda, in control of a new state in the heart of the Middle East is a potential disaster, not only for the region but also for the Western countries whose citizens are fighting with ISIS and who, radicalized and combat hardened, can easily return home.

The border between Iraq and Syria is gone. Any arms sent to the rebel forces in Syria can easily end up in Iraq. Any arms captured by ISIS in Iraq can end up in Syria. A U.S. policy that supports and arms ISIS in Syria and fights ISIS in Iraq in completely dysfunctional and is doomed to fail. Any direct U.S.-on-the-ground military intervention risks making the situation worse rather than making it better. The regional powers, particularly Iran, are best positioned to understand and deal with the situation.

The Iranian Quds Force, having faced a similar situation with an incompetent Syrian Army and leadership, has a demonstrated ability to provide leadership quickly and address the problem. While Iran, aware of the risk of sparking a sectarian civil war, will certainly tread cautiously, the U.S. should be supportive of reasonable Iranian efforts to intervene. The U.S. should also pressure its allies, Turkey, Qatar and Saudi Arabia, to cut off the flow of arms into Syria and to cease support for rebels in Syria. Hezbollah and the Syrian Army have the ability to open a second front and force ISIS to transfer their limited forces to the west. The biggest national security threat to the U.S. and Iran in the Iraq/Syria conflict is the creation of two failed states and chaos in Iraq/Syria. In this war, Iran is our natural ally.

History and Ideology Help Us Understand the Jewish and Islamic States (Blog from 11/5/2014)

As the nation states established in the Middle East by the European colonial powers following World War I have begun to disappear, new self-proclaimed states are arising to take their place. The breakdown of the established borders began following World War II when, in November 1947, UN General Assembly_Resolution_181 recommended the establishment of an Arab state, a Jewish State and a Special International Regime for the City of Jerusalem with an economic union within the British Mandate of Palestine. The recommendation was accepted by the Jews, but was rejected by the Arab states and the recommendation was never implemented. In May 1948, the Jews proclaimed the independent state of Israel. War between the Jews and Arabs ensued. The 1949 Armistice agreements established the Green Line or "1967 borders" between the combatants. These borders lasted until the Six-Day War in 1967 when Israel conquered the Golan Heights, the West Bank of the Jorden River, Gaza and the Sinai Peninsula. These borders remained until the 1978 Camp David Accords, which returned the Sinai to Egypt. In recent years, Jewish leaders have begun to insist that the State of Israel, as presently constituted, be recognized as a "Jewish State."

Following the 2003 U.S. invasion and occupation of Iraq, al-Qaeda in Iraq (AQI) arose as a resistance organization against the occupation. The 2007 U.S. troop surge and the "Sunni Awakening" forced the remnants of AQI to decamp to Syria. The chaos of the 2011 Syrian Civil War allowed AQI to reconstitute itself as the Islamic State in Iraq and Syria (ISIS). Making effective use of Gulf State financial aid and captured weapons, ISIS in 2013 and early 2014, was able to eliminate the colonial border between Syria and Iraq and, in June 2014, ISIS leader Abu Bakr al-Baghdadi proclaimed the "Islamic State" (IS) in the territory ISIS had conquered.

It remains unclear what these proclamations mean in practical terms for people living in these states. Judaism has been a religion of blood relationship, tribe and place since Yahweh was seen as the God of the Israelites more than 2,500 years ago. One does not become a Jew; one is born a Jew. It doesn't matter if one is a diaspora Jew or a Jew living in Israel, for Jews, whether practicing Jews or atheists, Israel from Iraq to the Nile River is the tribal homeland. Since non-Jewish residents of Israel are not members of the tribe, defining the status of non-Jews in a Jewish State is a major problem for Israel's leaders. Until this issue is resolved, continued violence will be the order of the day in Israel. Currently the Israeli strategy appears to be one of making life so difficult for non-Jews that, in the words of Mitt Romney, they "self-deport."[30] Given the attachment of Palestinian Arabs to this same land, self-deportation is unlikely to be a successful strategy.

ISIS leaders, on the other hand, have a different problem. Islam, since its founding by the Prophet Muhammad, a member of the Quraysh tribe in Mecca, has been an inclusive religion that superseded tribal boundaries. In order to become a Muslim, one need only ascribe to *Shahada:* declaring there is no god except God, and Muhammad is God's Messenger. The uniting of the fractious, warring, nomadic tribes of the Arabian Peninsula created a fearsome Army of Islam that spread Islam throughout the Middle East and North Africa within a century. The ranks of Muslims expanded as Christians persecuted as heretics by either Rome or Constantinople found Islam an appealing refuge. Many Christians converted in order to be able to fight in Saladin's Muslim army against the Crusaders. As a result of this inclusiveness, Islam has grown today to 1.5 billion adherents. The Islamic State's problem is that the violent, intolerant version of Islam that it proclaims has very few followers and supporters in the greater Muslim world. Observers on the ground in IS-controlled territory report that fewer than 10 percent of the population subscribes to the ISIS view of an Islamic State. IS is able to maintain control only by threats of extreme violence and by delivering government services in areas wracked by chaos and instability. While IS is very good at recruiting disaffected youth as fighters, in the longer term, IS, given its philosophy that edu-cation should only include religious subjects, faces major problems in recruiting the technical skills needed to deliver services. Oil refineries, power plants and construction projects do not respond well to sermons. The extreme violence is also likely to wear thin with tribal leaders.

The Jewish and Islamic states face difficult, deep-seeded, ideology-driven problems that will be hard to resolve. Unless they are able to overcome these problems, the prospects for long-term viability are uncertain.

Will Obama Change Direction Just as His Policy Shows Signs of Succeeding? (Blog from 11/19/2014)

As the Western main stream media has focused its breathless coverage on the brutal murders of hostages and captives by the Islamic State (IS), it has largely ignored the first green shoots of progress toward containing the IS threat in Iraq. While the world has been trans-fixed by the videos of beheadings of hostages such as Peter Kassig, the Iraqi army, augmented by Iranian advisers, Shiite militias and U.S. air power, has quietly reclaimed several Iraqi towns such as Jurf al-Sakhar and Baiji from IS. These events, along with the ability of Syrian and Iraqi Kurds to create a stalemate in the Syrian-Turkish border town of Kobane, have managed to break the momentum of IS and to damage severely its aura of invincibility and inevitability.

Within the areas of Syria and Iraq controlled by IS, the brutal tac-tics used by IS to enforce its eighth century version of Islamic Law have begun to alienate many tribesmen. Residents of Mosul and Aleppo, who originally welcomed IS as a force able to bring order out of chaos, have begun to turn against the brutal IS system of governance.

While it is unclear what the Obama administration's strategic goals are in the campaign against IS and what "degrade and destroy" actu-ally means, the tactic to harass from the air and hope for the best actu-ally seems to be getting some traction. While this tactic has serious potential for unintended consequences of blowback from returning foreign jihadist fighters and families of those killed by U.S. air strikes, for now, it probably remains the least bad alternative. Containment of IS may be the best option.

If the U.S. goal of destroying IS means pushing it out of the territories that it has conquered in Iraq and Syria and restoring the colonial borders, significant ground forces will be required. The Kurdish Peshmerga and the Iraqi army will not be up to the task. The other alternatives are Turkey, Iran, Syria, Hezbollah and the United States. Turkey, concerned about the rise of Kurdish nationalism, supportive of its Sunni co-religionists in IS and seeing the Alawite-Assad regime in Syria as illegitimate, has been reluctant to get involved. Iran, concerned about turning the conflict into a sectarian war, deeply mistrustful of U.S. objectives in Iraq and Syria, facing the imminent breakdown of nuclear negotiations and benefiting from a U.S. quagmire, is also reluctant to directly engage in the American effort. The U.S., unable to engage with the Syrian regime or Hezbollah, is left with few palatable options.

At this point the U.S. seems to be committed to training the "moderate elements" of Syrian opposition and gradually increasing the U.S. "boots on the ground." Turning the Iraq campaign into another U.S. war in Iraq will play into the IS narrative of a Western war on Islam, eliminating any hope of wooing moderate and secular Iraqi Sunni tribesmen to the cause. All bets are off as to the outcome. Training 5,000 "moderate rebels" in Syria is an equally hopeless effort. Five thousand outside recruits stand no chance of competing with 30,000 plus hardened IS fighters.

Deploying U.S. forces into the middle of the current four-way Syrian civil war is a recipe for disaster. Such deployment would inevitably bring the forces into conflict with the Syrian military, either on the ground or with anti-aircraft missile sites. How Syria's allies, Russia and Iran, would react is anybody's guess. Given the current state of U.S.-Iran and U.S.-Russia relations, they are unlikely to react favorably. In the worst case, it could result in a region-wide conflict.

As the Obama administration, under pressure from war hawks and liberal interventionists, gradually escalates the U.S. involvement in solving the IS problem, the risks associated with this involvement also escalate. Better to realize that the solution to the IS problem is a Middle East regional political issue. The U.S. can help, but cannot solve the problem. There is no military solution to what, at its core, is a political problem.

Six Things You Need to Know in Order to Understand ISIS (Blog from 2/23/2015)

The Obama administration continues to struggle in its efforts to craft an appropriate response to the threat posed by the advance of the Islamic State in Iraq and Syria (ISIS). While Obama has declared that his goal is to "degrade and destroy ISIS," he has not gone much further in defining what that means in terms of formulating a strategy. The pontificating by neo-conservative and liberal interventionist pundits and politicians is not helpful and, in fact, is counterproductive. Any effort to create a coherent strategy that has much chance of being successful will require a realistic assessment of ISIS, its strengths, weaknesses and goals as well as a threat assessment as it relates to U.S. national interest. There are six things to keep in mind in this process:

1. ISIS did not arise in a vacuum. The milieu in which it arose was a powerful mold that has shaped its worldview. The conservative Salafist, takfiri brand of Islam, with its intolerant, rigid interpretation of Islamic law, which has been exported around the world by the Wahhabis in Saudi Arabia, has laid the ideological groundwork for the global support for ISIS. The U.S. invasion of Iraq and the subsequent bungled occupation and nation-building effort as well as the chaos of the Syrian Civil War were the triggers that set off the emergence of ISIS as a powerful faction. The majoritarian rule of the Shia government in Iraq, which alienated Iraqi Sunnis, contributed to the increased popularity of ISIS in Iraq and Syria and its growing military strength.

2. ISIS is a terrorist group and more. The term terrorist has been so misused that it has lost any meaning. For me, any group that kills civilians, intentionally or with reckless disregard for consequences in pursuit of political objectives, is a terrorist group. By this definition ISIS is a terrorist group. It is, however, also a criminal gang,

a political party and a proto-state. It extorts citizens, steals property, kills its opponents, spreads its ideology, manages and delivers services and dispenses justice. Any strategy that focuses only on the terrorist component and ignores the others is unlikely to be successful.

3. ISIS' global appeal results from deeply imbedded conditions in many countries around the world. Its popularity and ability to recruit followers depends on disaffected Muslim youth searching for adventure and Western Islamophobic actions and rhetoric that play into its message that Muslims are under attack in non-Muslim countries and that the only road to safety is to create an Islamic caliphate. Changing these conditions will be a difficult, long-term project.

4. ISIS is susceptible to declining support. Its conservative, violent ideology of "One leader, One authority, One mosque: submit to it, or be killed" is deeply unpopular in the areas where it rules. IS only remains in power through fear. While the violence and deprivation resulting from years of war have drawn many to become more religious, Iraqi and Syrian Muslims have long been secular. Sooner or later they will say "enough is enough" and turn on their oppressors.

5. ISIS is not a Syrian rebel group. ISIS' aspirations are transnational. The other Sunni rebel groups are a bigger threat to the goal of creating a Sunni Islamic caliphate than is the Assad regime in Damascus. The Assad regime is perfectly happy to have ISIS fighting the rebel groups whose objective is to overthrow the Syrian government. Having ISIS weaken the rebel groups, but remain in control of its current large, but sparsely populated region, would not be a bad outcome for Assad. The question for the Western powers and their regional allies is whether or not this is an acceptable outcome for them.

6. ISIS is a political movement, not a religious movement. While ISIS uses religious language to attract followers and justify its actions, its ultimate goals are political. Its terrorist actions, while they kill people, are political theater designed to achieve a political outcome. A counter-terrorism strategy alone will not defeat ISIS. A reaction against the larger Muslim community will be counterproductive.

The "degrade" part of "degrade and destroy" is the easy part. The current tactics of air strikes will probably accomplish this. The "destroy" part will be much more complicated and long term. I have seen no sign that the Obama administration has a strategy to achieve this.

CHAPTER 10

Rising Powers

Not only have regional players attempted to fill the growing power vacuum in the Middle East, but other external powers, particularly Turkey and Russia, have begun to insert themselves into this vacuum. Brazil, China and, to some extent, the EU, having interests in the region that need to be addressed and protected, also have begun to realize that they can no longer rely on the U.S. to protect their interests. Add to the nation states, the non-state actors such as Hezbollah, Hamas and al-Qaeda, and it becomes clear that the region has truly become multi-polar.

Russia, an emerging diplomatic force, has proved that it again is becoming a factor to be reckoned with, particularly with respect to the crisis in Syria. Russian Foreign Minister, Sergei Lavrov, has gone out of his way to demonstrate, not only that Russia is a reliable ally, but also that he, himself, is a very adept diplomat as demonstrated by his negotiating skills during the crisis over Syrian chemical weapons. President Obama, having previously drawn a "red line" on the use of chemical weapons and having threatened a military action that had little or no public support, found himself in an untenable political position. Lavrov was able to negotiate a diplomatic solution, defuse American efforts to orchestrate a military strike against Syria and pull President Obama's "chestnuts out of the fire." Once ISIS became a factor to be reckoned with, Russia, concerned about Syria becoming a failed state with the resulting risk of jihadist blowback into the restive Caucasus provinces, took aggressive military action in support of the Syrian government against ISIS and Syrian rebel forces. This action has begun to turn the tide in favor of government forces. The growing government success has forced the U.S. to reconsider its "Assad-must-go" policy and makes a diplomatic solution more likely.

Russia, by opposing increased sanctions and threats of a military attack on Iran, also has acted as a moderate counterweight to America's more belligerent stance on the Iranian nuclear program. These efforts will go a long way toward helping Moscow gain the trust of other regional states.

Turkey, on the other hand, has struggled to find its footing as a regional power. It announced a policy of "Zero Problems with our Neighbors" saying:

> Aware that development and progress in real terms can only be achieved in a lasting peace and stability environment, Turkey places this objective at the very center of her foreign policy vision. This approach is a natural reflection of the "Peace at Home, Peace in the World" policy laid down by Great Leader Atatürk, founder of the Republic of Turkey. Besides, it is a natural consequence of a contemporary responsibility and a humanistic foreign policy vision.[31]

In pursuit of the policy, then Prime Minister Recep Erdoğan and Foreign Minister Ahmet Davutoğlu traveled widely through the Middle East and other neighboring countries. When the Arab Awakening brought Islamist governments to power in a number of countries, Turkey's moderate Islamist governance was held up by many as an ideal model. In 2010, Turkey, in cooperation with Brazil, negotiated a fuel swap arrangement with Iran that had the potential to defuse the Iranian nuclear crisis. Although the U.S. had endorsed a similar deal six months earlier, it flatly rejected the Brazil/Turkey deal, giving Turkey a diplomatic slap in the face. When an international aid convoy of ships headed to Gaza was attacked by Israel, several Turkish citizens were killed. In response, Turkey broke off relations with Israel. When the Syrian uprising began, Turkey, feeling very self-confident after all the global attention, immediately inserted itself into the fray. Erdoğan, giving the rebels diplomatic support, providing refuge for fighters and a government in exile and allowing arms to flow through Turkish territory to the resistance groups, came down strongly on the side of the rebels. As the Syrian crisis deteriorated into a full-fledged civil war and al-Qaeda-linked groups gained the upper hand, Turkey, feeling pressure to help find a solution from neighbors who supported the Assad regime, was forced to reconsider its policies. The success by Iraqi and Syrian Kurdish militias in confronting ISIS resulted in the establishment of self-governing Kurdish enclaves along the border with Turkey adjacent to the Kurdish regions of Turkey. Worried about a rebirth of the Kurdish rebellion, Turkey began to see the Kurds as its most threatening enemy and focused its military intervention in Syria on weakening the Kurdish forces. Its, at best, ambivalent approach to the ISIS threat has had a negative impact on its relations with the western powers.

As a result of its missteps, Turkey found itself at odds with Russia, Syria, Iran, Egypt and Israel. Instead of "Zero Problems," the policy morphed into "Problems with everybody."

China, having endured years of occupation and economic interference by the western imperial powers, having observed the negative effects of colonialism on emerging countries and giving priority to dealing with domestic issues, has long made non-intervention in the affairs of sovereign nations a cornerstone of its foreign policy. Its default position is non-intervention. That said, as China's economic reach and interests have expanded around the globe, it has been forced to rethink and reframe its non-interference policy. With thousands of expat workers arrayed around the world, including the Middle East, and with a growing appetite for Middle East oil, developing the ability to project power overseas has become an imperative. In order to learn how to conduct military operations in other countries and cultures, China has deployed troops as part of UN peacekeeping missions. The People's Liberation Army Navy (PLAN) has participated in the UN-mandated anti-piracy operation in Somalia and has operated in the Arabian Sea and the Gulf of Oman.

Thus far, China has shown little interest in becoming directly involved in the myriad of disputes that characterize Middle East politics. It has largely confined its policies to opposing intervention in the affairs of sovereign states, protecting its access to natural resources and to markets for its goods and supporting Russia's efforts in the region. As I was told by a number of Chinese during my last visit, "We saw how the Soviet Union's involvement in the Afghanistan quagmire bled them economically and politically and resulted in the collapse of the state. We have no interest in going there." Only time will tell whether or not they can maintain this stance.

The other world powers, both established and rising will assert themselves to protect their national interests as they see them. U.S. policy makers will need to take this changing geopolitical landscape into account to a greater degree than they have in the past.

How We Got Here:

A Changing Middle East Landscape
(Blog from 4/7/2009)

As I write this, President Obama is winding up his first major overseas trip to Europe. The trip began with a flurry of summits including the G20, the European Union and NATO with meetings with various heads of state sandwiched in between. By in large he came away from these meetings with optimistic press releases, but little in the way of European commitments on the issues that were at the top of his agenda such as greater European assistance in Afghanistan and increased economic stimulus spending.

The final stop on the trip in Turkey has the potential to be more productive. This is the latest in a series of events, which began during his inaugural address and continued with his al Arabiya interview,[32] designed to reach out to the Muslim world. Judging from the response in the Middle Eastern media, he seems to be having some success.

Turkey, by virtue of its geographic location at the confluence of a number of American foreign policy interests and its status as a secular democracy governed by the modestly Islamist AK party, is uniquely positioned to be helpful with such issues as Russia, Iran, Syria and Israel/Palestine. Maybe the message to Europe is: "If you won't help, we will search elsewhere for someone who will."

But how will Israel react to U.S. efforts to improve relations with Arab and other Muslim countries? Israeli media pundits have not been all that happy. It is hard to see how the U.S. can be part of an attack on Iran at the same time it is conducting discussions aimed at stabilizing Iraq and Afghanistan. This leaves Israel to go it alone and, for incoming Prime Minister Netanyahu, this is job one.

I used to think that we would have advance warning of an Israeli attack on Iran by virtue of the fact that they would have to attack Lebanon first in order to neutralize Hezbollah and their massive missile arsenal, which is capable of inflicting enormous damage on Israeli population centers. It now appears that Israel has chosen to begin to prepare their population to cope with large retaliatory attacks by Iran, Hezbollah and Hamas.

Calculations like this don't seem to make much sense, but I guess, by now, we should be used to people in this region starting wars in the hope that something good will come out of them.

Whose National Interest? (Blog from 7/4/2010)

While I was traveling around China a few weeks ago, the Middle East and its neighbors were busy. During this time came the Israeli attack on the Gaza-bound aid flotilla (which resulted in the deaths of nine people, including one American), the startup of so-called "proximity talks" between Israel and the Palestinian Authority, and the U.S. full-court press for sanctions on Iran.

These stories were available in China, but were not front-page news. The Chinese press was more focused on floods and labor unrest. Added to that, the Chinese government's squabble with Google made it inconvenient to access Google-related web sites to post comments so I will recap:

The U.S. high-pressure effort to get the five permanent members of the UN Security Council on board for a new sanctions resolution on Iran was successful and the new resolution passed with only Turkey and Brazil voting against and Lebanon abstaining.

It is reasonably clear why China and Russia might support sanctions. The Chinese government is not going to do anything that is against Chinese national interest. In the case of Iran, China values its economic ties with the west and the sanctions have been so watered down that they will not affect China's economic relations with Iran. Russia also values its economic ties with the west and any action that might disrupt Iran's natural gas industry would enhance Russia's monopoly position on gas supplies to Europe.

What is less clear is why Europe and the U.S. would support sanctions. As noted above, one possible outcome is that Europe will be even more dependent on Russian natural gas and will be more exposed to being held hostage to supply cutoffs resulting from Russian pricing disagreements with Ukraine or Belarus.

The U.S. is engaged in two intractable conflicts in Iraq and Afghanistan. It is unclear to me why the U.S. would want to escalate its confrontation with Iran at a time when it needs Iranian cooperation in order to stabilize these situations. The stated purpose is to stop Iran's nuclear enrichment program. However, CIA Director Leon Panetta, recently said on ABC: "Will [sanctions] deter them [Iran] from their ambitions with regards to nuclear capability? Probably not."

China's policy is to defend its own national interest, whereas the U.S. seems to persist in taking actions in the Middle East that are not in its national interest. It seems to me that China will be more successful.

Success and the Iran Nuclear File (Blog from 5/23/2012)

P5+1 is a group of six world powers that, in 2006, joined the diplomatic efforts with Iran to discuss Iran's nuclear program. The term refers to the P5 or five permanent members of the UN Security Council, namely the United States, Russia, China, the United Kingdom, and France, plus Germany. P5+1 is often referred to as the E3+3 (or E3/ EU+3) by European countries.

With the convening today of the second meeting of the current round of negotiations between Iran and the **P5+1** (or the E3+3, depending on whether you are talking to Americans or Europeans) over Iran's nuclear program, there has been much discussion about whether or not these talks will be a "success." In order to get any kind of answer to this question, we need to define what "success" means and I think that it means something different to all of the parties.

For the Iranians, the primary objective is to normalize relations with the West and to have the U.S. recognize Iran's legitimate role in Middle East regional politics. Everything that Iran has tried to accomplish over the past decade has been designed to achieve sufficient negotiating leverage to obtain significant concessions from the P5+1, and to create a stockpile of enriched uranium that can be used as a bargaining chip in any negotiations.

Defining "success" for the P5+1 or E3+3 is a more complicated endeavor, since there is little agreement among the parties on what success looks like. For the European countries (Britain, France and Germany) success is obtaining an agreement with Iran that ensures that Iran does not develop nuclear weapons and that modifies any sanctions so that Europe is assured of a continued flow of oil to the weak European economies. Russia and China share the goal of no nuclear weapons in Iran, but differ in their approach. Russia, as an oil exporter, is comfortable with the ongoing confrontation as it drives up the global price of oil. China, on the other hand, is an oil importer and desires a return to normal commercial ties with Iran.

The U.S. is an even more complicated situation as there are numerous powerful forces influencing policy decisions and thus preventing a united position. The Obama administration would like to "kick the can" past the elections and, in the interim, lower the tensions in order reduce the price of gasoline. To this end, the U.S. has quietly signaled to the Iranians that it would accept low level uranium enrichment. Also, according to an Iranian political analyst close to the government, the U.S. recognizes that the Iranians consider the threat of military attack as a "bad joke," and has signaled that the military option is no longer on the table.

The Israel lobby and its allies in Congress, on the other hand, see "success" as regime change in the Islamic Republic and are taking steps to blow up any negotiations, and maybe the region as well. By large majorities, both Houses of Congress have rushed through legislation that will tie the Obama administration's hands in the give and take of negotiations and are also taking steps to remove the Iranian terrorist group **MEK/MKO** from the U.S. terrorist list, a move that will enrage all Iranians.

MEK/MKO is an Iranian leftist revolutionary organization that participated in the 1979 Revolution that overthrew the Pahlavi Shah.

My definition of "success" is much more modest. I would be pleased if we just managed to schedule another meeting.

The State of Play in Syria (Blog from 1/23/2013)

Since the diplomatic agreement orchestrated by Russia to destroy the Syrian chemical stockpiles has moved forward, the bloody civil war in Syria has receded from the front pages of the western media. Despite this lack of media coverage, the war and the killing have proceeded apace. With the hysteria surrounding chemical weapons gone, now might be a good time to examine the state of affairs in this unfortunate country.

Observers on the ground in Syria are reporting a dramatic change in the capability of the Syrian armed forces.[31] When Hezbollah and the Iranian al-Quds Brigades forces arrived on the scene a year or so ago, they were appalled at the state of the Syrian Army. They found that it was poorly led, undisciplined and more designed to repress the ordinary Syrian citizens than to fight an organized, well-armed rebel force. Today, the army is well led and motivated and has made significant progress toward recovering territory lost to the rebels in the early days of the rebellion.

While some of their supply lines from Jordan and Lebanon have been cut by the Syrian Army, the rebel armies are being resupplied through Turkey with arms, ammunition and reinforcements by Saudi Arabia and its western allies. The reinforcements consist of Sunni jihadists recruited from around the globe including in the U.S. and the U.K. Many of these militants have been trained in Jordanian training camps financed by Saudi Arabia. The fact that there have been mergers and alliances between opposition groups reflects not unity, but division into competing camps with some of them allied with al-Qaeda. The al-Qaeda connection, combined with the fact that some of the fighters are British and American citizens with the ability to travel to and from their native countries, is worrisome to policy makers.

With this worry in mind, international politics is moving more in the direction of the Assad regime. Western powers are beginning to see Assad as the lesser of two evils with European countries exploring the possibility of reopening ties to the Syrian government. Since Russia saved President Obama from himself by negotiating a diplomatic solution to the chemical weapons issue and taken military action off the table, the U.S. has gone from a policy of "regime change" to "no policy." The U.S. appears to have outsourced its Syrian policy to Russia. Sergei Lavrov and Vladimir Putin are taking the lead in the thankless job of resolving the Syrian mess. With control of territory moving back and forth between rebel forces and the Syrian army, with life in Damascus being relatively normal (barring the occasional terrorist attack), and with divisions appearing within the rebel forces, the situation appears to be evolving into a stalemate.

Civil wars generally end in one of three ways: 1) One side wins and the war is over. 2) There is a negotiated agreement to allow power or territory sharing. 3) The war goes on until everybody is tired of the bloodshed and the fighting stops. With outside interventions, the possibility of one side winning appears remote. With the divisions within the rebel forces the idea of a successful peace conference is unlikely. The killing will probably go on for a long time, until both sides are exhausted.

Can the U.S. Deal With a Middle East Earthquake?
(Blog from 12/2/2013)

Over the last month, the geopolitical landscape of the Middle East has been jolted and fractured by the earthquake of the EU3+3 interim nuclear agreement with Iran, which allowed some relief from Western sanctions on Iran in return for limitations on Iran's nuclear program. The agreement set a six-month deadline for negotiations of a final agreement and can be extended by mutual agreement. Numerous political aftershocks have followed. The players who are wedded to the status quo are struggling to navigate this new landscape. Western and regional diplomats have been jetting around the region in an effort to figure out how to deal with the changes. This turmoil within traditional alliances has come at an inconvenient time for the Obama administration as it struggles to implement its announced pivot or rebalancing to the Pacific. As National Security Adviser, Susan Rice, told *The New York Times* in October, "We can't just be consumed 24/7 by one region, important as it is."[33]

Ever since the Vietnam War forced Richard Nixon to "pivot to the Pacific," the U.S. has, at various times, relied on strong regional allies to protect its interests around the globe. Initially in the Middle

East, the allies were Iran and Saudi Arabia. Following the Iranian Revolution in 1979, the U.S. relied on Israel, Saudi Arabia and, at times, Egypt. Under George W. Bush this "twin pillars" strategy was abandoned for a policy of direct unilateral intervention to protect U.S. interests. Now, just when Obama would like to rely on regional allies, the whole alliance structure is shifting and breaking down. The Egyptian Revolution has taken Egypt completely out of the picture.

Saudi Arabia's divided and dysfunctional foreign policy team, desiring to maintain good relations with the U.S. while supporting sectarian conflicts in Syria and Iraq, is being sorely tested. The Saudi's vehement anti-Iran policy and leadership in the Gulf Cooperation Council (GCC) are being challenged by Iran's diplomatic blitz. The Iranian diplomatic effort has led to a GCC invitation to Iran to attend the Manama, Bahrain Security Conference. Lebanon has rebuffed a Saudi suggestion that the Lebanese army turn its guns on Hezbollah, Iran's ally. The possibility of Iran dramatically increasing its oil production threatens the Saudi role as the swing producer in OPEC. Faced with the declining power of a key ally, the U.S. has relied on its default response of selling the Saudis billions of dollars of high-tech weaponry.

America's other pillar in the region, Israel, has its own struggles. The death of anti-apartheid hero, Nelson Mandela, came at a particularly bad time for Israel as it focused attention on Israel's treatment of its non-Jewish population and resulted in growing international criticism. Even the vaunted lobbying power of AIPAC is being called into question for its failure to prevent the Geneva Nuclear Agreement with Iran and, thus far, its inability to torpedo the Geneva agreement with new Congressional sanctions. As Obama's threat to veto any new Iran sanctions shows, Israel, with its intransigence with respect to settlements thus far torpedoing all of the Obama administration's Middle East peace initiatives, seems to be losing its influence in the White House. While the frustration with Israeli political pressure hasn't reached the level of George H. W. Bush when his Secretary of State James Baker infamously said "F**k the Jews, they don't vote for us anyway," the frustration is certainly increasing. With a second-term President who isn't facing an election, Israel has a problem.

While Saudi Arabia and Israel are discussing an alliance to counter

Iranian influence, it appears to be a marriage of convenience. As the U.S. attempts to back away from direct commitments in Syria and Afghanistan, it will leave a power vacuum. It is not clear who will be able to fill this vacuum. Russia and China have ambitions in the region, but they have neither the will nor the way to fill the U.S. role. As Beirut-based Alistair Cooke said in his recent post on Conflicts Forum, "Winding-down the U.S. commitment in the region does not mean that all the area's problems will be solved, but it does imply that the U.S. will no longer be expected to resolve them all."[34]

A Dose of Reality Arrives in Syria (Blog from 2/8/2014)

As the Syrian civil war drags on into its third year, it appears that the players, internal and external, in this long running tragedy may be starting to exhibit some common sense. With over 130,000 people killed to date on all sides, millions of people displaced internally and externally and the conflict gradually spreading into neighboring countries, leaders of the involved parties appear to at least be thinking about taking steps toward resolution of the crisis.

From the beginning of the conflict in March 2011, U.S. policies have been guided by geopolitical considerations involving Iran and Hezbollah rather than humanitarian concerns. Since Iran relies on Hezbollah to act as an asymmetric deterrent force against Israel and Hezbollah relies on Iran for financial and military support, if the conduit through Syria were cut off by the fall of Assad, both parties would be weaker. Israel, therefore, would be less deterred from attacking Hezbollah and Iran. Early on, many U.S. politicians, led by Senator John McCain, advocated for the U.S. intervention in support of the rebels. The Friends of Syria, which was made up of 114 nations, was formed by the U.S. and its allies and met numerous times in 2012-13 for the purpose of organizing military and other aid to the rebel organizations. Saudi Arabia and other Gulf States sent millions of dollars to jihadist rebel groups. President Obama confidently stated that, "Assad must step aside"[35] and told Iraqi President Maliki, "Assad will fall in two months."[36]

As the situation on the ground in Syria began to deteriorate in 2013, the external actors began to have second thoughts. The al-Qaeda-linked Islamist rebel groups usurped the more secular Syrian National Council and became the dominant rebel force. Western powers became concerned that their citizens fighting with radical Islamist groups would return home and bring the war to the home front. (According to intelligence sources, there are over 50 U.S. citizens currently fighting with jihadists in Syria.) The pro-Assad forces have regained territory from the rebels, and Iran, Russia and Hezbollah have been steadfast in their support for the Assad regime. The first Friends of Syria conference attracted 114 nations; the last conference attracted 14. The outside actors, with no good outcome in sight, have begun to search for a plan B.

While some of the suggestions for a plan B, such as reaching out to the al- Qaeda linked al-Nusra Front, are absurd, others being implemented and considered make sense. The U.S. and Russia organized a Geneva II conference, which included all sides of the conflict. While the U.S., unable to get over its animosity toward Iran, refused to allow Iran to attend, Secretary John Kerry reached out to Iranian Foreign Minister Zarif at the Munich Security Conference. Unsurprisingly, Zarif rebuffed his advance. Al-Qaeda leader Ayman Zawahiri has disowned the jihadist group Islamic State of Iraq and Syria (ISIS), seeing them as too radical. (Now that's a statement.) In what is perhaps the most important development, Saudi Arabia, under pressure from the U.S., has announced that it is abandoning its fighters in Syria and Iraq. Without Saudi support, it will be very difficult to sustain the jihadist armies.

Turkey's President Abdullah Gül has proposed cooperation among Turkey, Iran and Saudi Arabia on the Syria issue. Since these three are the main regional supporters of the protagonists, if the three can reach an agreement, a lot of pressure can be brought to bear to end the conflict.

The Russians are Coming (Blog from 10/8/2015)

Since the Syrian uprising began in 2011 and gradually morphed into a full blown, vicious, deadly civil war, U.S. policies toward the conflict have been affected by some of the faults that have plagued U.S. Middle East policies for over 50 years. When the uprisings began as peaceful demonstrations protesting corruption within the government, income and wealth inequality and lack of economic opportunity, the U.S. was faced with conflicting policy choices. On one hand the United States government could work with Iran to influence the Syrian government to negotiate with the opposition forces and to address their grievances peacefully (although unlikely given the state of U.S.-Iranian relations), recognize domestic political concerns and stay out of the situation, letting the Syrians solve the problem for themselves, or weigh in on the side of the rebel factions in hopes of overthrowing the Syrian government and thereby weakening Iran and Hezbollah and reducing the threat to Israel. The Obama administration decided to try and balance the last two alternatives, providing some support for the rebels, while not committing enough American troops to effectively change the facts on the ground.

Continuing its practice of trying to find "good guys" among the myriad of fractious and diverse opposition groups who would become its proxy army, the U.S. tried to organize, equip and train the Free Syrian Army (FSA). This endeavor was a complete failure as, after spending millions of dollars, the number of troops in the field can be counted on one hand and most of the trainees, arms and equipment have ended up in the hands of jihadist Islamist groups. As the policy gradually fell apart, the conflict deteriorated into a stalemate.

Enter the Russians. Unencumbered by conflicting policy goals, having only the objectives of keeping the Syrian government in power, willing to work with regional allies such as Iraq, Iran and Hezbollah, concerned about violent Islamic groups spreading to the homeland, seeing ISIS as its primary adversary and able to rapidly deploy troops and fire power, Russia seems to have quickly affected the facts on the ground.

In fact, Russia already has expanded and upgraded the Syrian Air Base at Latakia allowing it to conduct over 35 strikes against opposition forces in the first week in October compared with fewer than 10 for the U.S. The establishment of a no-fly safe zone along the Turkish border with Iraq and Syria requires the establishment of air superiority. When Turkey agreed to allow U.S. planes to fly combat missions from Incirlik Air Base, the quid pro quo was that the U.S. would turn a blind eye to Turkish air strikes in Iraq and Syria. In the first weeks of strikes, Turkey attacked ISIS three times and Kurdish positions over 300 times. The presence of Russian forces and aircraft greatly complicates Turkey's plans to establish a safe zone. This presence also increases the risk of conflict between Russian and Turkish forces. Since Turkey is a member of NATO, there is risk that the U.S. could be drawn in. Most observers expect coordination among Russian, Iranian, Syrian and Hezbollah forces in a major offensive prior to the onset of winter.

The shift in the power dynamic could portend a move toward a negotiated settlement. Iran and Russia now have considerable influence with the Assad government. The U.S. seems to have changed its position on Assad being a party to the negotiations, and abandoning its "Assad-must-go position." An Allied offensive against the rebels may bring them to the table with a unified, more flexible position. Negotiated endings to civil wars are rare, but one can always hope. In such an event attention could turn to solving the ISIS problem.

CHAPTER 11
A Way Forward—
Reversing the Decline

Over the past hundred years, the U.S. Middle East policy has evolved from complete disengagement to "all in." The beginning of American involvement came after the founding of Israel as a home for the Jews, and when the geopolitical landscape in the region looked considerably different than it does today. In 1948, the Sykes-Picot construct, created by the colonial powers during World War I, still held sway. But the events of the 21st-century Arab Awakening have made it plain that this artificial construct never evolved into a social contract between the governed and the government.

Since the U.S. began its interventions in the Middle East region, we have seen its influence rise to the pinnacle of power and influence in 2003 before beginning its precipitous decline. At the peak of its influence, the U.S. was able to topple unfriendly governments and install governments that it saw as supportive of its interest and policies. The U.S. government had a vision that these new democratic governments would not only be friendly to the U.S., but also provide an example to other Middle Eastern states. Other states would follow suit, form democracies and remake the region into the "new Middle East."

Iran, fearing that it was next on the target list, looking for a way off of the list, and, eager to negotiate a rapprochement with the U.S., tried to open the lines of communication with the Bush administration. As the *Washington Post* reported at the time:

Just after the lightning takeover of Baghdad by U.S. forces three years ago, an unusual two-page document spewed out of a fax machine at the Near East bureau of the State Department. It was a proposal from Iran for a broad dialogue with the United States, and the fax suggested everything was on the table—including full cooperation on nuclear programs, acceptance of Israel and the termination of Iranian support for Palestinian militant groups.

But top Bush administration officials, convinced the Iranian government was on the verge of collapse, belittled the initiative. Instead, they formally complained to the Swiss ambassador who had sent the fax with a cover letter certifying it as a genuine proposal supported by key power centers in Iran, former administration officials said.[37]

Feeling extremely confident, the Bush administration never replied. When I asked a former senior State Department official why the U.S. didn't explore what seemed to be an historic opening, he told me, "We didn't think it was real." For American decision makers, events did not work out quite as well as planned.

Instead of being welcomed as liberators, U.S. troops faced fierce resistance and a decade-long insurgency in both Iraq and Afghanistan. Thirteen years after being at the peak of its power, the U.S. is faced with a far different Middle East landscape than policy makers envisioned in 2003. Not only are traditional regional competitors becoming more assertive and new adversaries appearing on the scene, even many of its traditional allies pay little attention to America's preferences and policy objectives. How did this happen? And, so quickly?

Despite the Obama administration's announced intention to "pivot to Asia," the Middle East remains vitally important to America's economic and security interests. The U.S. is uniquely positioned to be a positive force for improving the security situation in the region and the lives of ordinary citizens. Notwithstanding all of the missteps over the past 60 years, in my experience, Middle Easterners genuinely like Americans. They admire and respect the values and principles that America stands for. While they may dislike the U.S. government and many of its policies, they see Americans as kind and generous. While they may quarrel with what they see as American's excessive individualism, they see America's principles of democracy, free speech, free press and economic freedom as principles that should be emulated in their countries. Even with America's traditional adversaries, such as Iran and Syria, this view prevails among ordinary citizens. Although some Middle Easterners would say that, since America is a democracy, American citizens are ultimately responsible for the policies of their government, I think this largely positive view of America and Americans provides a base on which to build policy formulations that restore America's influence in the region.

U.S. Policy Objectives

As is the case with any sovereign nation state, the U.S. has, during the years of its involvement in the Middle East, tried to shape events in ways that support what it sees as its national interest. While these interests have varied somewhat over the years, in general terms they can be put into five categories:

1. Access to stable supplies of oil at reasonable prices

2. Support for the state of Israel

3. Preventing adversaries or potential adversaries from coming to power or achieving influence in the region

4. Improving life for the people of the region (this objective has probably been honored more in the breach than in fact)

5. Preventing terrorist attacks on U.S. territory and citizens

In many ways, these national interests are affected by events in a territory that is larger than just the Middle East region, but, because the region occupies such a critical geopolitical position, its importance to realizing these national interests is heightened.

The region straddles the traditional trade routes among Asia, Africa and Europe. For this reason, it has always been a region of conflict. From the time of Cyrus the Great and Alexander the Great, major powers have competed for control and influence. In the 21st

Century little has changed. Although trade is no longer conducted on camels along the Silk Road, the dynamic of the Middle East as a trade crossroad still exists. We, in the West, and particularly in the U.S., are used to seeing the globe through a lens that has America, Europe and the Atlantic Ocean in the center of the world. Who in my age cohort cannot remember sitting in a classroom in which a Mercator projection map hung on the wall behind the teacher? This projection showed North America and Europe as the center of trade, and as larger than areas closer to the equator and the Atlantic Ocean. This image has framed the worldview of generations of Americans.

With the rise of Asia, the 21st-century reality is that the world looks more like this, with the Middle East and the Indian Ocean at the center.

The modern states of the region, particularly the wealthy oil producing states of the littoral Persian Gulf, have taken advantage of this geostrategic position. The Middle East has become a hub for global finance, business, tourism and transport. Dubai's Emirates Airlines is establishing a hub system that sends the message, "You can fly anywhere in the world, you just have to change planes in Dubai."

The Middle East region also contains the holy sites of three of the world's great religions. The three monotheisms are exclusivist religions, believing that they alone are the source of ultimate truth. This dynamic leads them to compete with each other for dominance. They each tend to believe that God is on their side. Israeli Prime Minister Yitzhak Rabin once said, "It is important that we do not theologize this conflict, because in religion there is no compromise."

The region has also become the epicenter for terrorist groups, some of which have ambitions for a global reach. While most of the militant Middle Eastern non-state actors have a local or regional agenda, some, namely al-Qaeda, ISIS and a few of their affiliates aspire to drive the "Western imperialists" out of the *dar al-Islam* (the House of Islam) and reestablish an Islamic caliphate. Since much of the world's petroleum-based energy resources are concentrated in the Middle East, the Middle Eastern producers have enormous influence over global energy prices and thus on the economies of the world. Everything that happens in the Middle East affects much of the rest of the world, politically, economically and religiously. In the view of the Western powers, particularly the U.S., the Middle East is much too important to be left in the hands of Middle Easterners.

Where Do We Go From Here?

As America has attempted to retain its influence and dominance in the region, some of the same issues and dynamics that have plagued U.S. administrations in the past have continued to haunt policy makers today. Middle Easterners, with their colonial history, are very sensitive to issues of national sovereignty and are protective of their political independence. In pursuit of what they see as America's national interest, policy makers have failed to recognize that other countries have their own national interests. They are not going to willingly submit to outside pressure or compromise these interests.

At times the perceived national interests of the U.S. have been in conflict with one another. It has become clear in the case of the U.S. interest in containing the Soviet Union or, as is the case today, containing and weakening Iran, the policies required have come in conflict with other interests. Confronting the Soviet Union adversely impacted relations with oil producing Soviet allies and resulted in destabilizing countries such as Afghanistan. Efforts to weaken Iran have prevented steps needed to resolve the Syrian Civil War and to end a humanitarian disaster. Uncritical support for Israel has damaged relations with other important Middle Eastern states. Is there a way to deal with this?

Making Choices

In my view, the solution to this ongoing problem of conflicting interests lies in one of the most difficult issues facing politicians and public figures, making choices. As a global power the U.S. has national interests around the world that require U.S. involvement at various levels. Not all of the interests of the U.S. are equal. The category that leaders should focus on is "vital national interest." My definition of a "vital national interest" is when, if left unattended and unresolved, presents an existential threat to this country's security, economic well being and way of life. Vital national interests are such that the country is willing to spend its wealth, put its citizens in harm's way and make a national commitment to dealing with these issues. Failure to make these distinctions and commit the necessary political capital to mobilize the nation behind a major effort to defend our vital national interests is a recipe for failure. Consider the case of Israel. While the U.S. and Israel have longstanding cultural ties and so-called "shared values," one should at least ask the question as to whether the security or lack thereof, of a small country on the other side of the world is really an existential issue for America; an issue that requires an all-out commitment of American lives and resources? One might even make the case that, absent unflinching support of its patron, Israel would have long since needed to make the difficult compromises necessary to reach an accommodation with its Arab neighbors. The promise by the U.S. of unflinching support for Israel, whatever its actions or behavior, creates a moral hazard. Israel takes on more risky actions, knowing that it has the world's superpower backing it up and shielding it from adverse consequences. This scenario has the potential to draw the U.S. into conflicts in which it has no national interest.

With the advent of new drilling technology, the U.S. is becoming a major producer of petroleum products. This is a complicated subject, but it raises the question of whether the maintenance of stable Middle East oil supplies is still a vital national interest. The U.S. has long since demonstrated that improving the lives of the people of the Middle East is a "nice to have," but it is not a vital national interest.

The issue of dealing with terrorism and terrorists is more difficult and controversial. The September 11 terrorist attacks triggered the actions and events that began the rapid decline of American influence in the Middle East. It was not the events themselves, but the U.S. responses to the events that were the issue. While the 9/11 attacks were a horrific tragedy for those involved, a source of dislocation for those living and working in New York City and Washington, D.C., frightening for Americans in general, and a temporary economic disruption for the rest of the country, in the broader scale of things these events were not an existential threat to the U.S. A few hundred jihadist fighters living in tents in Afghanistan were not going to destroy the U.S. and its way of life. The U.S., however, reacted as though this were an existential threat. Had the Bush administration stepped back and carefully considered the appropriate response a lot of physical and economic pain—physical, economic and other, might have been avoided.

It seems that the Bush administration learned a lesson from unintended consequences of its responses. Following the 2008 attacks in Mumbai, India which originated in Pakistan and which killed 164 people and wounded many others, Secretary of State Condoleezza Rice flew to India. She put enormous pressure on Pakistan to "respond robustly," but counseled India not to attack Pakistan. The potential consequences of a major war between these two nuclear-armed adversaries were too great to contemplate.

Whichever side one comes down on regarding the most important interests in the region, the actual choices of which are most important, still need to be made. Whatever choices are made obviously will have consequences.

Recognizing the New Realities

One thing that I learned during my business career is that the first step toward solving any problem is to recognize the brutal reality. Wishful thinking and rose-colored glasses will not get it done. While the U.S. remains the most powerful external actor in the Middle East, we must realize that other regional power centers, state and non-state, have become increasingly assertive in promoting their own interests. America needs to acknowledge that it no longer has the clout it once did. If America wishes to retain influence, it must cooperate with others, both inside and outside of the region. The days of "go it alone" or "my way or the highway" are over.

Another reality that we must acknowledge is that the region is rapidly changing and the future will not look like the past. Any attempt to replicate past policies is doomed to failure. Success will depend less on traditional measures of power and more on relationships with partners and on diplomacy.

Former Ambassador Chas Freeman pointed out in a 2013 speech to the National Council on U.S. Arab Relations (NCUSAR):

The simple world of colonial and superpower rivalries is long vanished. The notion that one is either 'with us or against us' has lost all resonance in the modern Middle East. No government in the region is prepared now to entrust its future to foreigners, still less to a single foreign power. So the role of great external powers in the region is becoming variable, complex, dynamic, and asymmetric rather than comprehensive, exclusive, static, or uniform. There is room for new as well as old players, but all will dance to tunes composed in the region, not in their own capitals or those of other outside powers...the Arab uprisings, revolutions, and coups of the past two-and-a-half years have repeatedly demonstrated that, for all our unmatched military power, Americans no longer command the ability to shape trends in the Middle East. Almost no one now expects us to do so. Delusions of imperial omnipotence die hard, but the question of the day is no longer how we or other outside powers will act to affect the Arab future. Both colonialism and neocolonialism are no more. For better or ill, the states of the region have seized control of their own destiny. ما شاء الله (masha›Allah God has willed)—and good luck to them![38]

To start crafting successful policies, the United States is going to need to rediscover diplomacy. For many years the U.S. has defined diplomacy as non-military coercion. As the U.S. became the world leading power following World War II, it increasingly relied on a "carrot and stick," threat and reward approach to dealing with its adversaries. The U.S. approach to negotiations has often been: you accede to what I want and then we can talk about what you want. During the 2005 round of negotiations with Iran over its nuclear program, the U.S. refused to talk to Iran until it suspended nuclear enrichment. Iran's response to this carrot and stick approach was that the "policy may be suitable for a donkey but not for a proud nation." There is no evidence that human beings react positively to threats. This applies to nation states as well. After a decade of threats, assassinations, cyber-attacks and sanctions against Iran, all to no avail in achieving the goal that Iran's nuclear program remain peaceful, the U.S. and its allies were forced to change their approach and revert to diplomacy. After months of intensive negotiations, Iran and the P5+1 reached an agreement limiting Iran's nuclear program and imposing an intrusive inspection regime in return for sanctions relief. While nobody was happy and hardliners on both sides have attempted to torpedo the agreement, that's the way it is with negotiations. In my business experience, the best deal is when everybody goes away mad.

The approach that the U.S. and its negotiating partners have taken in dealing with the Palestinian Islamist group, Hamas, during the on-again, off-again Arab/Israeli peace negotiations has been "Hamas cannot be part of any Middle East peace talks until it recognizes Israel, renounces violence and abides by agreements previously signed between Israel and the Palestine Liberation Organization." In 2008, Khaled Mashal, the political leader of Hamas, told me, "We will never renounce our right to resist occupation, but if Israel withdraws to the line of 1967, the resistance is finished." The talks have been stalemated for decades.

On the other hand, during the successful peace talks in Northern Ireland, mediator George Mitchell took a different approach. He did not force the IRA to *renounce* violence in order to participate in negotiations. Instead he said that the IRA had to *declare* a stop to violence. The IRA could go back to violence if negotiations didn't work. This brought everybody to the table and led to a peace agreement. Establishing unrealistic preconditions is a recipe for failure.

Ambassador Chas Freeman addressed this as well in his NCUSAR speech saying,

> We need to rediscover diplomacy. By this I mean something radically contrary to our recent militarism and the related concept of 'coercive diplomacy' through sanctions...Diplomacy, like the successful management of interpersonal ties, lies in the replacement of zero-sum problem definition with frameworks that promote the recognition of common interests. It presupposes empathetic, if reserved, understanding of adverse points of view. It incentivizes good behavior. It avoids vocal denial of the legitimacy of the other side's interests. It relies on convincing the other side that its objectives can best be achieved by doing things our way, and that it's in its own interest to change its policies and practices to do so. We seem

to have forgotten how to do diplomacy in this sense. At least, it's been a long time since we tried it in the Middle East.

Another tool in the diplomatic toolbox that needs to be rediscovered is "soft power." Soft power according to Harvard Professor Joseph Nye (who coined the term), is getting others to want what you want. According to Nye, a country's resources of soft power are, "its culture (in places where it is attractive to others), its political values (when it lives up to them at home and abroad), and its foreign policies (when others see them as legitimate and having moral authority." It goes without saying that American culture, for better or worse, has infiltrated almost every country around the world (with the possible exception of North Korea). More can still be done by promoting cultural and academic exchanges.

When it comes to living up to its values, however, the U.S. is frequently seen as a hypocrite. Espousing values of democracy, human rights, freedom of speech and press and rule of law while at the same time supporting brutal dictators, carrying out extrajudicial targeted killings, practicing indefinite detention without trial, conducting torture and implementing massive surveillance does not contribute to soft power. Foreign policies that produce poverty and human rights abuses do not lead people to respect the U.S. In order to enhance soft power the U.S. needs to practice its values and principles at home and abroad. This doesn't mean that America can or should impose its values on other nation states, but instead stand up for the values that have made America great with friend and foe alike:

- Democracy—people have a voice in their governance

- Free speech

- Freedom of religion

- Free press

- Independent judiciary

In addition to articulating these principles, American policy makers need to make ethics and morality part of the conversation. As my friend, Ambassador Todd Stewart, said in his essay on Just War, "Ethics deserves more attention by practitioners of international relations. Without ethical guideposts that have been worked out in advance by an individual, institution or society, a decision maker easily lapses into situational-ism where self-interest is all too easily justified. Law, medical and business schools now offer, and sometimes require, courses in ethics...I am not aware of any organized discussion of ethical issues in the Department of State or, for that matter, any other foreign ministry. The absence seems strange in the light of the importance of the decisions in foreign affairs." States need to decide for themselves what kind of a state they want to be. The best America can do is provide an example and not facilitate or exemplify bad behavior.

Nye also coined the term "smart power" which he described as a strategy that "denotes the ability to combine hard and soft power depending on whether hard or soft power would be more effective in a given situation." This concept has been adopted by liberal interventionists, such as Hillary Clinton, to justify coercion and military intervention to accomplish policy goals. However admirable the goals may be, it is hard to get people to "want what you want" when you are sanctioning or bombing them. Smart power and soft power may be mutually exclusive.

As Ambassador Freeman has also pointed out, "We cannot afford to assume that the future will resemble the past in the Middle East. Whatever it looks like, it will certainly differ from what we have seen over the past century." The problem is that the Washington establishment insists on playing by the old rules. By "Washington establishment," I mean the whole panoply of executive, legislative, State and Defense Department and intelligence government officials who craft American foreign policy. In addition, I include the military-industrial figures, foreign and domestic lobbying groups, media pundits and think tanks that exert enormous influence over foreign policy decision makers. In the 21st century environment, U.S. policy makers must rethink what it means to lead.

Following World War II, with the U.S. the only power left standing, the concept of the "American Century," a term first coined by Henry Luce in 1941, began to have credence with U.S. government leaders. The idea that the U.S. and *only* the U.S. can lead and transform the world and that it has an obligation to do so became grounding principles of American foreign policy. This idea has become so ingrained in orthodox U.S. foreign policy thinking that, no matter which political party is in power, the impulse for interventionism is the standard. The neo-conservative wing frames intervention in terms of spreading American values and the neo-liberal wing frames intervention in terms of humanitarian principles. As we have seen, the urge to intervene has brought the U.S. into conflict with the desire for national sovereignty by countries newly freed from colonialism.

The founding fathers of the American experiment had a deep distrust of a standing army and the idea of a citizen army that could be mobilized as needed was the governing principle of national defense. As the Cold War began, American leaders began to define national security, rather than improving the lives of citizens, as the primary task of the federal government and the standing army became the norm. In 1973, the draft was eliminated and the U.S. reverted to an all-volunteer, professional mercenary military. The development of a professional military class, many from generational military families, subjected to multiple lengthy deployments, feeling the physical and emotional pain of death and injury created a separation from the average citizen who is comfortable ensconced at home and insulated from the pain and suffering of conflict and war. The result is that elected politicians feel little pressure to avoid conflict.

In the 1990s, the U.S. adopted the two Major Regional Conflict (MRC) construct as the basis for sizing the military forces. The confluence of these two norms led to the development of a military sized all out of proportion to the requirements for national defense.

Top Five Defense Budgets—2012
(budget authority in billions of current U.S. dollars)

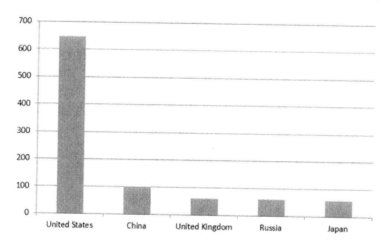

Foreign policy began to be based more on military power and other forms of coercion rather than **multilateralism** and diplomacy. This national security strategy requires a global military presence and ability to project power around the world. The need for this global presence has led to the U.S. establishing 600-700 military bases, depending on how you define a base, on foreign soil. In comparison, Russia has 12, the U.K. has six, France has six, Turkey has one and India has one. The ubiquitous presence of American bases has at times been welcomed on foreign soil as big-spending Americans help local economies. At other times American bases have been unwelcome and a source of conflict with countries. The fact that the African Command is based in Stuttgart, Germany is a good example of this outcome.

Multilateralism is multiple countries working in concert on a given issue. Multilateralism was defined by Miles Kahler as "international governance of the 'many.'"

As the old cliché goes, when your only tool is a hammer, every problem looks like a nail. When government leaders, with few electoral constraints, have an overpowering military advantage, there is a strong tendency to use it. Madeleine Albright, Secretary of State under President Clinton, is a classic example of this phenomenon when she said to the Chairman of the Joint Chiefs of Staff, "What's the point of having this superb military that you're always talking about if we can't use it?" Confidence that the U.S. can go anywhere and win any conflict reduces the likelihood that American decision makers will see the necessity for diplomacy.

Again, Ambassador Freeman has some good advice. "We must acknowledge the reality that we no longer have or can expect to have the clout we once did in the region (Middle East). The practical implication of this is that we must cooperate with others—strategic competitors as well as countries with whom we are allied in other contexts—in order to serve our regional partners' interests as well as our own. The United States remains the most powerful external actor in the Middle East, but American primacy has been slain by the new assertiveness of the region's inhabitants. If we give others space to displace us, they will." As such, Americans in general, and policymakers in particular, must rethink what global leadership means. Arkansas Senator J. William Fulbright had this to say, "Maybe we are not really cut out for the job of spreading the gospel of democracy. Maybe it would profit us to concentrate on our own democracy instead of trying to inflict our version of it (on others)." And, "I think that the world has endured about all it can of high-minded men bent on the regeneration of the human race. (Any people setting out upon) self-appointed missions to police the world, defeat all tyrannies to make their fellow man rich, happy and free (are more likely to) wreak havoc, bringing misery to their intended beneficiaries and destruction on themselves."[39]

All this said, one might well ask, what is the likelihood that America will change or adjust the policies and principles that have led to the precipitous decline in American influence in the Middle East and around the world? The answer unfortunately is, not likely. As Andrew Bacevich observes in his book *Washington Rules*, he notes: "The Washington rules are likely to remain securely in place for the foreseeable future. Or they will until the strain of a military that is perpetually at war and on an economy propped by perpetual borrowing causes one or the other to collapse."[40] Two factors play into this situation.

One factor is bureaucratic inertia. Many of the senior policy makers, pundits, think tank leaders and lobbyists have grown up in a post WWII era in which, as the only major power left standing after the decimation resulting from the war, the U.S. was the global super power and was able to exert its power (military, diplomatic and financial) in order to coerce or cajole other nations to accede to its policy preferences. Even President Obama, who has taken a much more multilateral approach to foreign policy issues than many of his predecessors, has used the phrase "American exceptionalism" more than any other president. Following the collapse of the Soviet Union, the U.S. became the global hegemon and saw its role as spreading liberal governance and economic policies around the global. The mantra became "if only you will become like us, the world will be a more stable and peaceful place." We will write the rules and you will follow them. The problem is, not everybody wants to be like us. In a multipolar world in which there are a number of power centers, U.S. policy makers will need to adapt. Policies that worked in the past will no longer be effective.

In today's Washington political environment, changing a long-entrenched policy formulation is very difficult. Military bases and military-industrial plants are conveniently spread around the country in many states and Congressional districts. Any policy that closes bases and plants can be portrayed as a job killer. Defense Department research funds are liberally distributed among major U.S. research universities. **Interventionist** policies are deeply ingrained in America's political and think-tank culture. There is consensus in the mainstream foreign policy establishment that America is special and unique and, therefore, has an obligation to intervene to change the world for the better. As Benjamin Friedman pointed out in a *Foreign Affairs* article, "...the foreign policy establishment consists almost entirely of neoconservatives on the right and liberal internationalists on the left. Realists and other reliable skeptics of intervention are essentially confined to the academy, while true isolationism has become virtually extinct in Washington."[41] Any policy maker who

Interventionist is a political term for significant activity undertaken by a state to influence something not directly under its control. It is an act of military or economical intervention that is aimed for international order, or for the benefit of the country.

advocates for a less assertive and interventionist policy is immediately branded an isolationist or appeaser.

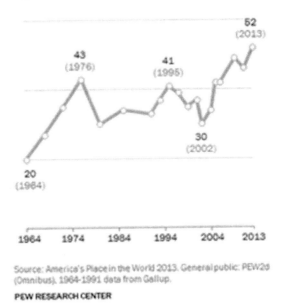

Majority Says U.S. Should 'Mind Its Own Business Internationally'

% agreeing that 'the U.S. should mind its own business internationally and let other countries get along the best they can on their own'

Source: America's Place in the World 2013. General public: PEW20 (Omnibus), 1964-1991 data from Gallup.

PEW RESEARCH CENTER

A second factor is that national leaders are immune from the electoral consequences of their foreign policy actions. As a 2013 poll by the Pew Center for the People and the Press made clear, the American people have an increasingly dim view of foreign interventions.

How can it be that, in a mature democracy, there is such a disconnect between the people and the governing elite. Friedman postulates, "People's foreign policy preferences rarely determine their decisions when it comes to national elections. So political leaders—those in Congress and those vying for the White House—can generally buck the public on foreign policy without losing votes. It is not that politicians entirely ignore voters' foreign policy views. But, at least compared with tax and entitlement issues, politicians have considerable rope to pursue their own agendas. Only in rare circumstances, such as very unpopular wars, do voters hold politicians to account on foreign policy."[42]

America has frequently proved Winston Churchill right when he said, "We can always count on the Americans to do the right thing, after they have exhausted all the other possibilities." The path may be long and difficult, but an educated public can make a difference if it asks itself the question, "Why shouldn't policy makers, as they debate the way forward on the road toward restoring America's influence in the Middle East, think about a different path; a path that leads outside the box and away from the failed paradigms of the past?"

Notes

1. The Protocol of Sèvres, 1956: Anatomy of a War Plot, Avi Shlaim, Foreign Affairs 73:3

2. "The United States and the Middle East: 1914 to 9/11," Video/audio lecture series produced by The Teaching Company, Chantilly, VA, 2003

3. Michael J. Oren, Six Days of War, Rosetta Books, 2010, p26

4. Richard M. Nixon (November 3, 1969). "President Nixon's Speech on "Vietnamization"

5. George W. Bush, Decision Points, Crown Publishers, 2010, p396

6. http://articles.latimes.com/2004/jul/03/nation/na-statue3

7. CNN.com—Rumsfeld on looting in Iraq: 'Stuff happens'—Apr. 12, 2003

8. georgewbush-whitehouse.archives.gov/infocus/bushrecord/documents/Selected_Speeches_George_W_Bush.pdf p273

9. http://www.theguardian.com/world/2006/aug/28/syria.israel

10. http://www.aljazeera.com/archive/2006/07/200849132037797119.html

11. http://www.npr.org/templates/story/story.php?storyId=6586565

12. http://www.theguardian.com/world/2011/mar/17/
un-security-council-resolution

13. https://www.washingtonpost.com/politics/karzai-meets-obama-
to-discuss-us-drawdown-in-afghanistan/2013/01/11/b50c72ec-
5c03-11e2-9fa9-5fbdc9530eb9_story.html?hpid=z1

14. https://www.whitehouse.gov/the-press-office/2014/09/10/
statement-president-isil-1

15. http://www.huffingtonpost.com/2013/09/10/kerry-syria-
rebels_n_3901762.html

16. http://english.al-akhbar.com/content/khamenei-
negotiations-us-permitted-specific-cases%E2%80%9D

17. http://nationalinterest.org/commentary/americas-east-
suez-moment-9193

18. http://www.huffingtonpost.com/s-azmat-hassan/saudi-arabia-
security-council_b_4150605.html

19. http://nationalinterest.org/commentary/americas-east-
suez-moment-9193

20. Jay Solomon, Muted Response on Military Sparks Theory U.S.
Backs Coup, Wall Street Journal, July 1, 2013

21. Middle East Report No. 118, International Crisis Group, 12 Mar
2012

22. David Brooks, Defending the Coup, New York Times, 14 July
2013

23. "America's Place in the World 2013," Pew Research Center,
December 2013

24. http://www.brookings.edu/research/reports/2015/01/08-
american-opinion-poll-isis-syria-telhami

25. http://i2.cdn.turner.com/cnn/2015/images/12/06/rel12d.-
.obama.isis.pdf

26. Alastair Crooke, THE TRUE SIGNIFICANCE OF AHMADINEJAD'S LEBANON VISIT, The Race for Iran, October 15, 2010

27. Aluf Benn, Obama team readying for confrontation with Netanyahu, Haaretz April 8, 2009

28. http://www.nytimes.com/2009/05/05/world/middleeast/05Meshal-transcript.html?_r=0

29. http://www.veteranstoday.com/2013/07/29/eu-having-buyers-remorse-on-blacklisting-hezbollah/

30. http://www.cbsnews.com/news/romney-on-immigration-im-for-self-deportation/

31. http://www.mfa.gov.tr/policy-of-zero-problems-with-our-neighbors.en.mfa

32. Hisham Melhem, Al Arabiya Interview. 27 Jan 2009

33. Mark Landler, Rice Offers a More Modest Strategy for Mideast, The New York Times, October 26, 2013

34. http://www.conflictsforum.org/2013/conflicts-forums-weekly-comment-6-%E2%80%93-13-december-2013/

35. https://www.whitehouse.gov/blog/2011/08/18/president-obama-future-syria-must-be-determined-its-people-president-bashar-al-assad

36. http://www.almanar.com.lb/english/adetails.php?fromval=1&cid=23&frid=23&seccatid=24&eid=82179

37. http://www.washingtonpost.com/wp-dyn/content/article/2006/06/17/AR2006061700727.html

38. Ambassador Chas. W. Freeman, Coping with Kaleidoscopic Change in the Middle East, Remarks to the NCUSAR 2013 Conference, October 22, 2013

39. J. William Fulbright, The Arrogance of Power. Random House, 2011

40. Andrew J. Bacevich, Washington Rules, Henry Holt and Company, 2010 p229

41. Benjamin Friedman, The State of the Union is Wrong, Foreign Affairs, January 28, 2014

42. http://www.cato.org/publications/commentary/state-union-wrong

Acknowledgments

At the beginning, I need to acknowledge the role Marcia, my best friend, traveling companion and wife of 50 years, has played in encouraging and collaborating to bring this project to completion. I must also thank my publisher, Mark Russell, and Elevate who helped me see the vision for this project and Anna McHargue, my editor, chief critic and manager of deadlines, who helped me to craft a coherent narrative from many years of writings and blog postings. Without you all, this could not have happened.

About the Author

Don Liebich is a native of New York and a graduate of the University of Rochester and the Harvard Business School PMD program. He spent his career with the U.S. Navy Nuclear Submarine service and Sysco Corp. After retiring from Sysco Corp, he engaged in numerous consulting projects in various countries including Russia, Poland, Czech Republic, Ukraine, Indonesia and Venezuela. He has traveled to the Middle East numerous times in the past ten years. Liebich has been involved with economic development, citizen diplomacy and human rights projects in Jordan, Israel/Palestine including the West Bank, UAE and Iran. He has conducted seminars and taught courses on Islam, Christian Fundamentalism, U.S. Middle East foreign policy and Iran. Don and his wife, Marcia, live in Hailey, Idaho. Don blogs regularly at www.donliebich.com.

elevate
publishing

DELIVERING TRANSFORMATIVE MESSAGES
TO THE WORLD

Visit www.elevatepub.com for our latest offerings.

CPSIA information can be obtained
at www.ICGtesting.com
Printed in the USA
LVOW12s2148220616

493734LV00012B/137/P